Subtle Mercies

Bob Fairchild

To my Lord and Savior Jesus Christ through Whom all things are possible.

To my parents, Bob and Anita Fairchild, who set an example of life and godliness before me.

To my bride, April Fairchild, who inspires me daily to be a man of god.

To my children, Kevin, Miranda, and Alyssa. Each of you has been my greatest accomplishment in life.

To my grandchildren, who fill me with joy and hope.

Contents

Introduction

Shortly after becoming the Senior Pastor at Covington First Assembly of God, the Lord spoke to me in my prayer time and said, "I have placed books in you." This was a funny statement because I was the kid who refused to read a book throughout elementary and high school. It wasn't because I had trouble reading but because I was too busy doing other things. It was difficult to get me to sit still long enough to listen to a story, let alone read one. Now, God was calling me to write. It's a good thing I fell in love with reading once I became an adult and was no longer required to read by a teacher. I accepted the Father's promise and tucked it away in my heart. I wasn't sure what He would have me write, but I was willing to obey His leading whenever He nudged me to get started.

Time passed, and I assumed He was waiting for me to do something, so I tried to write several times. I had no trouble writing sermons or Bible studies, but I could not write a book. Each time I tried to put a thought down, I ended up staring at a blank screen on my computer. My attempts ended with frustration, failure, and questions. I wonder if Abraham felt this way too. He had received a promise from God, became impatient, and produced Ishmael instead of the promise he had hoped for. One thing is for certain; I did not want to write a book on my own strength because it would be a very short and uninformative book. So the desire to write a book went on the shelf for several years, pun intended. I let go of the idea of "producing" a book and trusted God with what He had said to me initially.

In the Spring of 2016, I was at District Council, and the Father asked me a question. He asked, "Do you want Me to give you Covington?" My response was, "Of course!" He spoke again and said, "Then put the soles of your feet on the city, and I will give it to you." Please understand that this is not a call for me to accomplish something great but for spiritual advancement in my community. I love my hometown. It is an honor to minister in the community where I grew up and among the people I love. I had been praying for this community for the previous twelve years in my prayer closet, but now the Lord was calling me out to the streets.

As I mapped out my path, I decided to go through the park to pray for the next generation. I wanted to go past the courthouse to pray for our local, state, and federal governments and past the schools to pray for our kids, teachers, faculty, and administrators. More was developed in these prayer walks that I will share at a later time. However, my path was set, and I continued to walk it faithfully, even today. I have walked in daylight and darkness. I walked when it was cold and hot. I have walked in the snow, and sometimes I have been rained on. Recently, the Holy Spirit challenged me that if people can sit in the rain for sporting events, I can also pray in it. A rain suit will be purchased soon because of this challenge.

Much of what I have written in this book has flowed from these journeys with Jesus. Each day I spend time with the Lord in prayer and meditation. His love is gently transforming me. I call these moments "subtle mercies" because they have become so commonplace it is like walking with a friend who is joyful to meet with me on every occasion. I am not referring to our Creator God as though He were somehow less than Who He is. I cannot make Him greater or less because He is immutably perfect. Still, just as Jesus lived among the disciples, I find His Presence is with me daily. He laughs with me and comforts me when I weep. He teaches me and corrects me when I need it. He truly is "God with us." It is in these moments that I have found the greatest spiritual transformation.

On one prayer walk, the Father challenged me to purchase journaling Bibles and write in them for my family. I had never been good at journaling, so I disciplined myself to obey the Father. I read the Bible throughout the year and prayed over the one I was journaling for daily. Then, I would write what I felt the Father impress on my heart from each day's reading. Once April and my children had a Bible, I started to journal different things the Father had spoken to me on our prayer walks together. Even in this, I wanted to record what He has spoken to pass on to my children and grandchildren one day. I had no idea that my daily discipline was producing the promises of God in my life.

In the Spring of 2022, I was near the courthouse on my prayer walk when the Father reminded me of His promise that He had placed books in me. I argued with Him. With the skill of a defense lawyer, I pleaded my case. It was fruitless. He explained that I had not been able to write because my heart was to write at an academic level to impress others. Yes, I have issues. You will see that as you read. I find myself identifying with the disciples in many ways. Still, the two I identify with most are the fact that I am "unschooled and ordinary" but that I, too, "have been with Jesus" (Ac. 4:13 NIV). This reality has been the core of my spiritual development. While I am a life learner, my education did not come through sitting under the direction of a professor but from sitting at the feet of Jesus in personal prayer and study. My path has been a little unorthodox, so my writing might be a little unorthodox too.

For this reason, I could not write anything to impress anyone but to "testify about what I have seen and heard" (John 3:11 NKJV). Thankfully, God is gracious to deal with me as needed. He did not want me to write from this pride-filled stance but from a perspective of humility. After I had received His affirmation, He said, "Besides, you've already written it. It's your prayer journal."

I was halfway through my prayer walk when He said this to me, and I had difficulty focusing the rest of the way. Once I returned to my office, I opened my journal, scrolling back to the beginning to reread what He had said at different times. My heart leaped as I was reminded of the glorious times I spent with my Heavenly Father in prayer and revelation. The writing came easy when I finally waited to let go of my ideas and settled on obeying Him.

The things I am sharing in this book are only a fraction of what I have recorded in my time of communion with Jesus. They are compiled here for my family first. You were on my heart as I prayed and wrote. You will find some family stories intermingled with some theology. I desire you to lay hold of at least the intimacy I have attained with this living God. However, don't stop there; go further! Exceed me in understanding! Go after Jesus with all you have and journal what He says to you too.

These thoughts are also compiled for anyone who reads them and finds inspiration. If you are from my hometown of Covington, know that many of these things were spoken to me as I prayed over you. Some of you see me walking and praying. Others of you have no idea who I am or what I am doing, especially in the winter months when I'm bundled up like an Eskimo. The Father loves you! He longs to spend time with you in sweet fellowship. I pray that these journaled thoughts will inspire you to seek His face for the first time or in greater measure.

If you are a stranger, knowing nothing of me or my hometown, you have also been prayed for. The names of my family, friends, and places mentioned in the following pages are nothing more than names to you, but the Jesus I write about is very near and knowable. My heart is to introduce you to Him so you might start your journey of sweet fellowship with Him.

Whatever you do, don't read alone. Invite the Holy Spirit to sit with you. Be inspired to journey with Him. Develop your own disciplines of study, prayer, and ministry to others. You are loved by God and useful for the Kingdom.

Chapter One

Subtle Mercies

I wouldn't change one ounce of my childhood. I lived at the corner of West Salem Church Road and Crowder Road, northeast of Covington, Indiana. Our house was small, and seven of us lived in it. My four sisters and I were blessed with the world's greatest parents. Being the "baby" of the family and the only boy has its perks, and I played it to my advantage as often as possible. I have always made jokes about having five women in the house and one bathroom. It was no joke! It was a reality that sent Dad and me outside often. In those moments, we were thankful for living in the country, surrounded by corn fields.

My family didn't live in luxury. Robin Leach, the host of the 1980s television show *Lifestyles of the Rich and Famous*, never knocked on our door to interview us or tour our home. However, we lived in a house that was rich in love and faith. It was proven by every meal prepared, each outburst of laughter, and every correction received. We were blessed and unaware of it at the time. Subtle mercies were everywhere.

The Christmas celebrations in our home were magical. I remember being awakened by my sisters while it was still dark outside. Since I was the "baby," Mom and Dad would get out of bed for me. With the manipulation of the finest salespersons, Lora and Paula prodded me into the dark room to stir Mom and Dad awake. Once we were given approval, we walked into the living room to find it full of boxes covered in brightly colored wrapping paper. Under the floodlight of Dad's eight-millimeter video camera, we tore into those gifts as if someone had fired a gun for a horse race. We did this not knowing we were establishing a lifelong tradition that we would later describe as "joyful chaos."

My grandparents, McKinley (Mack) and Rebecca (Becky) Fairchild were our nearest neighbors. North and west of their house was an eighty-acre farm that I called "my playground." While the house may have been crowded and loud, on that farm, in the woods, my "playground" was where I could explore the vast regions of boyhood uninterrupted. Well, at least until I could hear the dinner bell calling me back for some well-prepared meals. Yes, that's what I said, a dinner bell. You could hear it from anywhere within that eighty-acre farm. At times, the bell would cease, and you could hear my grandma's voice yelling in the moments of silence, calling us in like we were one of the cattle in the pasture. On occasions when I was out too long, it was my mom's voice yelling with it.

If there was ever a comparison in my mind of what the Garden of Eden must have been like, that farm had to be close in resemblance. There was even a small field in the westernmost part of the woods that my dad referred to as "Heaven." To get to it, you had to take the tractor through the woods, across a creek, and up a hill before it opened up to the one-acre patch. I always felt like it was too much trouble to get back there with the machinery, but it was Dad's favorite field to work. He loved the seclusion and the beauty of it.

There was a greater harvest in his heart as he worked that field than there ever was in crops harvested. That property and "Heaven" had been subtle mercies to my father before me. He had grown up in those woods, exploring and playing just as I had.

My grandparents started going to Florida for the winter, probably to escape us. Sometime in the early 1970s, another tradition was started. We were loaded into the station wagon and driven to Robinson Orange Park in Plant City, Florida (or "Old People Park," as I lovingly referred to it). We loved this trip because we got a dose of sunshine in the wintertime, and spending the week with Grandma and Grandpa Fairchild was a treat for all of us. Most days were spent outside in the warm Florida climate. My sisters would lay out to get a tan while I rode Grandma's three-wheeled bike, often on two wheels, around the loop of that retirement community. I befriended a man named Bill, who had two small dogs. They provided me with entertainment as I played with them and placed them in Grandma's tricycle basket for rides. Oranges were picked from the orange grove, shuffleboard was played, and strawberry shortcake and ice cream were devoured at Parksdale Farm Market. It was far from a five-star resort, but we wouldn't have known. One day would be spent at Disney World and another at Clearwater Beach for the day my dad termed "Fry Day." Like Christmas, this trip would come once per year, and just as quickly as it came, it went. The weight of goodness found in those times has carried over to my family and my siblings' families. We may not go to Robinson Orange Park anymore, but Redington Beach has served our family well for over thirty-five years.

Every day could not be Christmas or vacation. As much as I enjoyed those extraordinary times, I was not shaped by their extravagance or luxury. These were highlights and had a role in my childhood, but they did not make me who I am. What shaped me the most were those subtle mercies of everyday life, moments so obscure to our memories we cannot even describe them. These subtle mercies took place daily, over time, through genetics and learned behavior. These moments were the clay-marred hands of my life; molding attributes in me unaware. These things were never imposed on me, but like a sponge, I absorbed them by mere geography, by being in the room and being present with my family.

When I was a teen, my mom watched me walk next to my dad on the way to the barn. She told me later that we walked alike. What? How could I walk like Dad? I hadn't tried to walk like Dad. It just happened, I guess, through genetics and having learned how to walk by watching him. I've walked and talked with Dad a lot. I remember walking with him to the barn when the snow was too deep for my little legs. That day I let him clear a path for me, stepping from one giant foot imprint to another until we reached our destination. I fell once, and he grabbed me back to my feet. Another time when I was a teenager, I had a walk and talked with him at about the same spot, only it was Fall. There was no snow, leaves were on the ground, and the subject matter was about a girl. That girl would become my bride one day. I was wavering a bit, but his words caught and steadied me much as his hand did in the snow all those years before. Looking back, I can't even name all the times we have gone on adventures together, whether to the beach, the Farm Progress Show, or the Indianapolis Motor Speedway. Anytime I was with my dad, or my mom for that matter, my life was filled with subtle mercies that formed me.

Lamentations says, *"Through the LORD'S mercies we are not consumed, Because His compassions fail not. They are new every morning; Great is Your faithfulness." (Lam.* 3:22-23 NKJV) God's faithfulness is not expressed to us on special days alone; it is an everyday faithfulness. He isn't faithful only when we are aware and can acknowledge it; He is faithful even when we think He is not. More than once, I have been like Jacob, awakening from his dream, saying, *"Surely, the Lord is in this place, and I did not know it" (Gen. 28:16 NKJV)* The subtle mercies of Heaven are all around us daily and at every moment, molding and shaping us, just as being near my parents shaped who I am. We tend to make one day or place more special than the other. No doubt, there are moments of extraordinary encounters with the Holy Spirit. I remember my camp experiences as a child, where I surrendered to Christ for salvation, the baptism of the Holy Spirit, and received a call into ministry at fourteen. Those moments were powerful. They were my spiritual Christmas and vacation, but I couldn't live there. I longed for more spiritual encounters filled with emotions and requests for more from God. In my immaturity, I wanted to make everyday life like these great moments.

I quickly became like Peter on the Mount of Transfiguration when he suggested building three tabernacles – one for Jesus, one for Moses, and one for Elijah. Peter had plans to stay there, but Jesus had other plans. He knew there was a boy down the mountain that needed a demon cast out. He knew Peter needed to walk with Him in seemingly less glorious places. Jesus knew work needed to be done in Peter before His ascension. Peter was amazed at the experience of Jesus' transfiguration, but it did not complete the work. He wasn't even allowed to talk about it at that time. All that was needed was for Peter to keep following Jesus, staying close to His side, and absorbing all He poured out.

I have learned that His mercies are truly new each morning. However, they are subtle. Like when I learned to walk by watching my father, my spiritual walk has taken on the gait of my Heavenly Father through daily observations. Yes, those extravagant encounters have played a role in my life, but they are not the source of my transformation alone. Daily, I get out of bed and discipline myself to gaze upon Jesus by studying His Word and prayer. I have found that He meets me every morning. Just as the mist would come up and water the Garden of Eden for sustenance, so does the Lord flood my soul as I walk with Him in the cool of the day. When I am on my prayer walk around the streets of Covington, those who drive past have no idea that I am communing with the Creator of the universe. Some honk and wave. Others don't even look in my direction. It doesn't matter if they see me because my Heavenly Father sees me. Just as manna would show up in the dew of the morning for Israel, so does the Bread from Heaven show up with me as I seek Him. While I appreciate the extravagant and luxurious encounters of church services or conferences, I have been shaped chiefly by the daily, subtle mercies of my Heavenly Father. Each day He has some new whisper for my heart.

I encourage you to seek out a disciplined prayer life for yourself. He is calling you beyond the church, beyond the lights and smoke of this culture's worship services, into a daily routine of fellowship. It is here that He will mold and shape you into His likeness. Be patient as you seek Him. Watch and listen carefully and see He has a subtle, still, small voice of mercy to speak to you today.

Chapter Two

A Quandary of Cherry Trees

I walk past two different cherry trees on my prayer walk each morning. With the wet, humid Spring we have had, the trees are full of ripe and ripening fruit. The atmosphere has set the tree to fullness, with bright red invitations to come and taste. Here is the issue. Though full and inviting, these two trees sit in two forbidden areas. One is very near the street but on private property. The other is on public property, at the northwest corner of the elementary school, but behind a fence. It is very near the fence but behind it nonetheless. When I walk past these trees each Spring, my mind and taste buds go back home, where I had two cherry trees to enjoy. I had full access to both trees and received many blessings from them.

My grandmother had such a cherry tree. It was rooted in the western part of her yard, behind the house. I suppose it belonged to my grandfather too. Still, Grandma always picked, cleaned, and cooked those cherries into delicacies that even a French pastry chef could envy. The other tree was located in the southwest corner of our yard. It was my mother's tree. I say "mother" because, like Grandpa, my dad never touched it. Mom would harvest those sweet and sour treasures and, like my grandmother, make pies that were perfect with a dollop of ice cream. Though we were country folk, we understood what cherry pie "a la mode" was.

Those trees were easily accessible. I could walk across the gravel road to my grandparent's yard, where I was welcome and encouraged to go. Of course, the one in my yard was accessible because it belonged to my parents. Until a ladder was raised against either tree, I could walk by and eat any low-hanging fruit I could reach. Like the local birds, I could have a taste whenever I liked, and it was free. When I did, though, I knew this little berry was good, but it was nothing compared to what some sugar and a pie crust would bring.

The harvest was always bountiful. Pails of cherries were washed, pitted, bagged, and frozen as they awaited their turn in flaky crusts made with hands of love. We ate the harvest as pies were made immediately by my mother. Others were stored only to reemerge for special treats and holidays to come. Still, others were being stored with the intentionality of being given away to families in need. For some, it would be a gift to celebrate a newborn baby. Mom would give others to those undergoing surgery or others who had experienced the tragedy of death. When placed in the hands of godly women, the cherries from these two trees were not only sustenance for the owner's families but gifts to others they loved.

As I remembered these precious moments, and my mouth watered for some of Mom and Grandma's pies, I realized the impossibilities before me. Though full of fruit, these trees I have walked past end the season in fruitlessness year after year. The cherries ripen and fall to the ground. What a disappointment! These cherries were designed by God to be eaten, yet they fall aimlessly to the ground each year. The first tree is accessible, but I do not have permission. It is not my property, and I do not know who to ask. Even if I did know who to ask, I would not have the confidence to ask out of fear of rejection. The other is on public property, yet behind a fence. It is barricaded off from me. I do not want to give an appearance of trespass. So, both trees will drop their fruit once again. If only these owners could place a sign saying, "These cherries are free. Help yourself and be blessed". They would be gobbled up quickly, no doubt. However, the barriers remain intact.

While contemplating all of this, my mind went to the church. It, too, is a tree that has grown from a seed of faith in this community. It is public and open for anyone to come and receive her fruit. I must wonder, though, do our neighbors around us question if they are welcome? Do they fear the possibility of being turned away? Do they fear that they might be seen as a trespasser walking through the doors? Do they have sweet memories of another church where they used to enjoy sweet fellowship with the Lord and others? Longing to experience it again in a new community, as an adult, seeing the potential of our church, why do they continue to walk by in admiration only? Perhaps there's a fence we have built unaware? Perhaps there's a property line they have not been invited to cross?

The church was designed to bear fruit for the Kingdom. The fruit of the Spirit should be in us and available to everyone we encounter each day. The fruit of the Spirit is not for us but for others, those around us, and those in need. These neighbors should be allowed to draw from our love, joy, peace, patience, kindness, goodness, faithfulness, gentleness, and self-control. May we harvest and glean from each time of worship only to present the fruit of the Spirit to others in the flaky baked crust of mercy and lattice of grace. May the fruit in our lives bring life to all who receive it. May it change their countenance, but most importantly, may they see the source that it is, a Tree of Life, Jesus Christ. Invite them to the "Source" that He is! While true evangelism is more than an invitation to join us for church, an invitation is a great place to start. It is an invitation to at least come to the "Tree" with you. Afterward, it's up to them to receive. All are welcome!

Why were these trees planted? My Uncle John Layton or his parents would have planted the one in the yard on Park Avenue. Of course! This tree had the same intentionality as my grandmother's tree. From family knowledge, that seed was planted, knowing the abundant fruit of blessing that would follow. That seed or sapling was planted, watered, and tended with the harvest it would produce in mind. Family pies and community blessings were its original purpose, but now it stands to drop its fruit alone.

What happened? I know that after my Uncle John's parents died, the house became a rental property. Several families have lived there over the years. Then, it was sold at least once and maybe more. I don't know for sure. Somewhere in all the property owners' transitions, the tree's original purpose was forgotten by those who could have tended to it. What was once a tree planted for the blessing of its fruit has now become a tree with untapped potential. Why is it untapped potential? Is it because the tree has stopped producing? NO! Not at all! It is because the tree's purpose is no longer valued. Since there is no value in the fruit it offers, it is fruit-filled yet dormant, except for the birds of the air.

And what about the other tree? Why might it have been planted? Since it is located on the school property, one can assume it was planted where it is for educational purposes. The tree's location is interesting because it is located in the furthest area away from the children. The northwest corner of the schoolyard, until recently, has been chiefly uninhabited by children. This area had no toys, slides, or swings. It had a somewhat organized backstop that the kids could use for kickball, but it was seldom used. The tree's location was even at the furthest corner of the least used property from any door. How could any child find it? Why here? What is educational about an unreachable tree? What benefit is its fruit if only to look at from afar but never taste?

In these two stories, I see the church again. The first is of forgotten purpose. Proverbs 22:28 (NIV) says, "Do not move an ancient boundary stone set up by your forefathers." While this is wisdom, churches often do move away from their foundations. If you took the time to study a church's history, you would find a mission statement somewhere. Nothing exists without a purpose. Churches that forget why they exist are churches that let their fruit fall to the ground. They become mausoleums that remember the life it once was rather than houses of worship that are alive today with hope for tomorrow. The countryside is sprinkled with them. You can find empty church buildings all over. We used to mock the great citadels of Europe for their beautiful architecture but empty pews. They are cherry trees that are admired for their structure alone, fruitless, other than to be gazed upon and toured, void of any life-giving quality. Any church that has forgotten who they are can be sure people have noticed them, but they are doing nothing to impact their lives.

The tree in the schoolyard is a result of a misguided planting. While someone had the vision to educate the children, it was planted with the wrong purpose. It was placed where the children or no one could ever eat the fruit. At best, this tree may be noticed in bloom, but it is overlooked at harvest. We all know that the best way to learn is to *"Taste and see that the Lord is good" (Ps. 34:8 NIV)*. I was the worst at rejecting education which seemed to have no purpose in life. Geometry, for example, received no effort from me until I realized it had a life application. I was all about application. If it appeared to have no application to life, I had no care to know it. I'm not saying this was right; it's just how I was as a child. There is nothing worse than education without an application. Young people go to college to get degrees that have limited value. They go into mountains of debt for a degree that is not marketable in the real world. They observed a tree for the wrong reason. They know all the systems but never tasted the fruit! This is religion. It teaches us about religious systems without life-giving fruit. What good is knowing without experiencing?

Taste and see. That is the life experience of the church. Come, taste the Love of God, see Him, educate yourself in Him, and experience fellowship with Him! The result is "goodness," which demands more goodness, just like multiple pieces of cherry pie! However, the church that exists with a legalistic, separatist mentality boasts of its structures but invites no one to experience God's goodness. They are walled off to be admired from afar and only visited by the birds of the air. May it never be said of our church that we have lost our purpose or have become misguided in what we have been called to do.

And what could be said of the onlooker? It is a chore to pick, clean, and pit the cherries. It takes effort and experience to achieve the perfect recipe for a pie. One must have the proper ingredients, tools, and pans to attain the full value offered on those trees. The trees aren't grocery stores. They are not commercialized or advertised for readymade pies and jams. NO! They are not bought but harvested with time and effort. Does the fruit remain and fall to the ground simply because it is easier to purchase a pie out of the freezer section of the grocery? Do they remain because a premade crust and some canned fruit are good enough? We all know that canned cherries and pie fillings are nothing like those picked fresh from the tree. If you don't know that already, I pity your lack of knowledge because you do not understand what you are missing.

Wait! That's it! The fruit hangs on those trees from ignorance as much as an inconvenience. If our ignorance was impacted by truth, we willingly inconvenience ourselves because the value of those cherries would exponentially increase. If we had indeed tasted and seen that the Lord was good, we would leave behind the convenient pie crust and canned fruit for the real thing! We might recognize the treasure we have found and purchase the property it was sitting on so that it could become ours for keeping. That sounds like Jesus' parables about the "Pearl of Great Price" and the "Treasure Hidden in the Field," doesn't it? Is the fruit of our churches in America falling to the ground because the culture would rather have an easy, commercialized religion that requires no effort on their part? Are they unwilling to sell out completely to Jesus because they are looking for a "bargain Jesus" that allows them to have all the world offers as well? It is easier to sit in a service and call it faith rather than take the time to dig into the Word of God for ourselves.

Spoon-fed baby Christians enjoy perpetual childhood. They can't reach the first branch of the Kingdom and have no desire to, especially if someone is willing to pick it, clean it, pit it, prepare it, and feed it to them once per week. Too many people prefer to lean solely on the efforts of their pastor for their spiritual sustenance. Like a mother bird gets up early to find the worm, eats it, and later regurgitates it in a form her chicks can receive, so do churches wait for their pastor to nourish them from the nourishment he or she has found in the Word throughout the previous week. I have told our congregation that I am willing to get up every day and seek the face of God for "a Word." I will be faithful to absorb it and then regurgitate it on Sundays. They may enjoy what I offer but never realize the "worm" tasted better the first time. When they learn to find their own "Word" from the Lord, they will have tasted and seen the Lord's goodness in a new way. As long as the church in America settles for the cheap, convenient religion of our day, we will never understand the joy of harvesting truths from the Word of God for ourselves and then passing on those truths to others.

Here I must confess. I stepped onto the property, reached the closest cherry I could, and harvested it. I enjoyed the fruit's flesh but stuck the seed in my pocket. I plan on having a tree of my own to bless others.

Chapter Three

Deep Calls Out to Deep

At the writing of this chapter, April and I are a couple of weeks from celebrating thirty years of marriage. We were nineteen years old when we were married on July 12, 1992. Beyond salvation, she has been the greatest blessing in my life. I don't know where I would be without her. It all began when we were fifteen years old. We met at her uncle's house, west of Covington. They had agreed to host a party for my youth group, and I went even though I had just had an emergency appendectomy. My body was still leaking the infection from an open wound on my side. Nothing is more humbling than knowing there's a beautiful girl in front of you and you're wearing a *Maxi Pad* on your side because your mom ran out of gauze. We learned to improvise on the farm; if there was ever anything we had in abundance, it was feminine hygiene products.

I looked across the yard that day, and I had no idea I was setting eyes on my future bride for the first time. While recording these memories, I took a selah moment, pictured that day one more time, and considered its magnitude. God is so good! Despite my sickness, He ensured I would be there to meet her that day! Not only that, He protected me. When released from the hospital, the doctor asked if I owned a trampoline, and I said, "no, why?" He said it would be the worst thing I could do to my body. I didn't ask about the consequences of doing so because I didn't have one anyway. However, there was a trampoline at the party, and this beautiful girl asked if I wanted to jump on it with her. Let's just say I seized the moment. At one point, the maxi pad fell off, and I threw it into the yard before she could see what it was. Shortly after this day, we were "official." Today there is a sign in our home with the exact longitude and latitude of where I was standing the moment I saw her that says, "where it all began."

I am thankful for that moment, but I am more grateful for every moment after. We began to grow toward one another and together. Like a magnet drawn toward ferrous metals, our souls began to long for one another until, finally, we were inseparable. April has been a gentle tool in the hand of the Father as He continues to mold and shape me after His image. I have learned the more sacrificial I love my bride, the more I grasp the heart of my Father. So many subtle mercies have been centered around my life with her. I want to share with you a good representation of that life. I have walked with April for over thirty years. In that time, as I have learned to love her more, the Father called me to deeper places in Him.

Over the years, one of our favorite summer destinations has been the Smoky Mountains in Tennessee. The Lord often speaks to me through nature, so these trips always prove to be very prophetic. On one visit, we decided to explore the Greenbrier area of the Great Smoky Mountain National Park. We had never been there before. We enjoyed a very secluded walk together. The trail was along a rocky stream and up a relatively comfortable graded hill. The walk was cool and quiet, besides the water and our conversation. It was special. As we visited, I also communed with the Lord in my heart. Being with April stirs me to worship, to a place of thankfulness and fellowship with God. I love her so much, and I am grateful for the precious gift she is in my life.

The trail would wind toward and away from the water as we walked. The further we got away from it, the more the sound would dissipate. The closer we got, the louder it sounded. At one point, I told April, "we are moving back toward the stream because it's getting louder." At that moment, the words "deep cries out to deep" went through my mind. I even spoke those words to her without explanation. The Lord had injected Himself into the conversation by impressing Psalm 42:7-8 upon my heart, *"Deep calls unto deep at the noise of Your waterfalls; All Your waves and billows have gone over me. The Lord will command His lovingkindness in the daytime, And in the night His song shall be with me— A prayer to the God of my life."* (Ps 42:7-8 NKJV)

The Psalmist had written this from a place of being downcast. He expressed his thirst for God as the depths of his soul longed for the depths of God's goodness and sustenance. I was not in a place of desperation at that moment, but I am always ready for the outpouring of the Holy Spirit in my life and through my life to others. I have practiced making sure my "deep" is answering the call of His "deep." That is not to say I have never faced dry seasons. I have! That is what makes these seasons of fullness and refreshing so special.

The stream we were strolling next to would beckon us. Whenever we were close enough, we would view it from every angle. Sometimes we were above it. Other times we were at its very edge, but every time it called, we came to it, soaking in its splendor for a few minutes. My mind continued to wander on these thoughts. The river of God daily beckons and calls for us to come to Him. If God is our Source and so many references to His provision are seen as rivers of blessing, we can draw from many different natural sources as examples.

This rocky stream was beautiful and calling to us only because it had rocks in it. Had it been a deep-flowing river, we could have been near it and not known because it would be silently moving in obscurity. This stream, however, was obstructed, and the obstruction became the testimony that made it cry out. Over every obstacle, it testified! Think of Jesus and the obstacle of the cross; it still speaks and calls people to a deep faith, deep belief, and deep transformation. There is no louder stream than that of the cross, where blood and water flowed, that stream of life-giving sacrifice. He calls to us, drawing all men to Jesus. Think of the rocks that were silenced by the praise of children before Jesus. If those innocent voices of ordained praise had been silenced by the religious leaders of the day, the rocks would have gained their voice of testimony to declare the goodness of God. I mused this reality and admired the cunning of the rushing sound next to me. The rocks in this stream worked in conjunction with the water flowing over them to bring a declaration of God that continues twenty-four hours a day. Even the rocks refuse to be silent, and like all creation, they declare something to us about our Creator.

What about those deep, quiet rivers? Is there no testimony? Of course, there is! They are constant. They are provisional, teeming with life. They are passageways for merchants and recreation. Just because they are not loud does not mean they don't have a voice. Think of John and the disciples of Jesus baptizing believers in the

Jordan. Even today, there are lines of people wishing to be baptized in those waters. You can find deep people like these rivers, who are constant, steady, and mappable. You don't have to search for them; they are right where they always have been. You don't have to search for their faith. It has never been empty and occasionally floods out of its bank. Deep streams are always full, and so are some people. It seems as if their lives are too easy without trials. The truth is this, their problems have been overcome, buried beneath the depth of God's grace. In a sense, they were cast into the sea of forgetfulness and remembered no more. Never judge a quiet, faithful believer. They are a deep river of faith.

What about wells? They are dug in dry places, deserts, and wastelands. Rocky streams call out. Rivers supply needs. However, wells must be sought by faith. A desperate seeker will say to themself, "If I dig here, I will find water." Every scoop of earth removed is done by faith, believing that if they do not give up, they will find the precious water of life they seek. Digging a well requires effort to find what is hidden in deep places. We dig deep while believing and being sure of what is not seen. I have often dug deep, looking for the Lord in dry seasons. I hoped to find something of God, not hearing or seeing that river, but by faith digging deep because He is good. Seasons of digging are not fun but praise God for the lessons learned in the hidden place of subterranean brokenness. So much faith has been stirred. So much trust has been developed. So much perseverance has proven faithful in maturing me. Thank you, God, for calling me to the effort of seeking you, and thank you for digging new wells in me.

What is the reward of these things? He fills us with rivers of living water! He fills us with Himself. We may be a "rocky stream" with a life seemingly filled with obstacles and a loud testimony. We may be a silent but deep river, full of life and baptized in spiritual strength. Still, others may possess the appearance of a rough and dry surface but have hidden refreshments found in deep wells they have faithfully dug in prayer and study. I've learned not to judge others based on outward appearance alone. I can learn something from everyone. So that which called to us also calls through us "deep calls to deep."

I have already spoken of how my bride stirs my spirit toward worship, but she is not the only one. I love when I find a brother or sister in the Lord, even if I don't know them. Our deeps cry out toward one another, and God speaks to us together. Just as deeps join together, so does the shallow. We must connect ourselves with those who have both drank the deep things of God and poured out those deep things as well. At the same time, we must make ourselves available to those seeking life and be the life they seek. Why? God calls us to deeper places in Him so we can lead others to those same depths of goodness. April has done this for me, and I pray I can return the blessing. In this, we can worship together until we finally do so around His throne.

Chapter Four

A Butterfly's Glory

One of the things my daughter, Alyssa, inherited from me is an insatiable curiosity for exploration and discovery. As a child, she loved to peer into the world of insects. We bought her a bug habitat for Christmas one year. It was a small plastic container with a painted green landscape. It came with a built-in magnifying glass for up-close observation. I often wondered what the bugs thought when suddenly, a giant and excited eye was looking at them. It must have been a special kind of torture during their captivity. Once in her possession, this dual-purpose chamber of death and joy almost always contained something. Her greatest accomplishment came when she heard about the metamorphosis of a caterpillar into a butterfly. She learned that if you place a caterpillar in the habitat with some milkweed, it will form a chrysalis and eventually emerge as a beautiful butterfly. Once the vision had been cast, the mission was set, and the search was on.

The journey to the hill behind our home was short, and milkweed was abundant. The weeds were inspected until a caterpillar was found. After imprisoning it into the bug habitat, she shoved some milkweed leaves in with it and waited anxiously. I was sure it would die like her past collections, but to my surprise, it didn't.

The little worm began to eat the leaves, and before long, it began its metamorphosis. With a very educated and passionate report, I was informed what to expect next with better accuracy than any weatherman could hope for.

The wait was finally over. She came home from school, and the first place she went was to look at her chrysalis with hopes of a revelation of a soon-coming metamorphosis. She waited like I could envision my father waiting outside the delivery room while my sisters and I were born. A yell came from her bedroom. "Daddy, it's dead!" I was met with genuine tears accompanied by what I assumed would be a corpse. However, there was no corpse. The top portion of the chrysalis was still hanging where it had been. At the same time, the bottom was gone and what lay below it was a slime made up of a few different colors.

What confounded me was the absence of what had been inside the chrysalis. Yes, it looked like a grotesque end to something, but where was the something? The caterpillar didn't just evaporate into a couple of drops of liquid. There was no half-formed butterfly on the bottom of the bug habitat, and there was no way a predator could have gotten in to eat it. At that moment, I moved from the role of comforting father to Sherlock Holmes so that I might investigate this crime scene for some answers. With keen observation, I thought to turn the habitat around. Okay, it wasn't keen. I just wasn't as emotional as she was, so I thought to look at the other side of the bug habitat. Then I saw it. A beautiful monarch butterfly was drying its wings on the backside of the scenic mountains within the little plastic dome. Alyssa's expression shot from tears of sadness to tears of joy and, eventually, amazement. We let this little miracle of God's glory dry its wings until they were rigid, and it was able to fly.

Alyssa took the butterfly outside, speaking to it the entire way like a mother would speak to her infant. She hadn't birthed this little insect, but she had cared for it deeply through its transformation. Once the little thing fluttered away, she laughed and wished it well. She wasn't sending her own child off into the world yet, but it was a small representation of what was coming for me someday. One day I will have to watch her flutter off into the world while hoping I've done enough to prepare her for it. Children must learn to spread their wings, and parents must learn to let them fly.

There is a more significant lesson in this metamorphosis. The story of Jesus is revealed throughout. The caterpillar eats the milkweed and then suspends itself from a leaf in a "J" shape as the chrysalis forms. After some time, it re-emerges as a butterfly, a sort of new creation. I often wonder if Alyssa's reaction was similar to the disciples' reaction to Jesus' death and resurrection. Suspended between heaven and earth, Jesus appeared to be finished. As He was cast into the chrysalis of His tomb, the heartbreak must have been agonizing. That pain was still present when they saw His body was missing, and they assumed someone had stolen it. Then the joy came! He is risen! What were once tears of loss turned into tears of joy, and the message of the resurrection of Jesus has not stopped being praised.

We will all face our own chrysalises in life. I think of the womb. The more we learn about the conception of a child in the womb, the more amazed we become at the miracle of life. When God blessed Adam and Eve, He commanded them to *"Be fruitful and multiply; fill the earth" (Gen. 1:28 NKJV)*. The miracle of life is a gift from God. Women were given a supply of tiny eggs, while men were given a microscopic seed to fertilize the egg. When the two are joined together, life begins, and in time the chrysalis of the womb brings forth a child that resembles the sources of its creation. The newborn child brings joy to all who see them. Pictures are taken. Birthdays are celebrated. The day the child comes forth will be remembered for all the days of their life.

What about the chrysalis of adolescence? What? Do you think there is no adolescent chrysalis? Take a moment to look back at your seventh-grade photo next to your senior picture. My seventh-grade photo frames a picture of a boy with curly hair. It would be one thing if the curly hair were natural, but it was not. Mom did her best. Still, my hair resembled someone who had stuck their finger in a light socket. So did the expression on my face. What happened to me in the next few years is what happened to each of us. We emerged from the chrysalis of Junior High School a little less awkward. I don't know if my family celebrated my transformation as much as they celebrated my birth, but no doubt there was some joy in knowing I would not be so awkward for the rest of my life.

What about the chrysalis of the tomb? The tomb is only a momentary chrysalis where our bodies will lie in wait for their transformation. The doctrine of the resurrection is as old as the curse of death. The book of Job is believed to be one of the oldest books in the Bible, yet we see Job prophesying about the resurrection multiple times. God did not leave us without hope! He spoke of it throughout the Old Testament, and He proved it with the resurrection of Jesus. When Christ emerged, He did so with a glorified body. We can be sure of the same promise for ourselves as we put our faith in Him. Will there not be a celebration when the dead are raised? Of course! What a glorious day for those who are in Christ!

What about the time between the two chrysalises of the womb and the grave? Many have pointed out the dashes between the birth and death dates on the headstones in cemeteries. The beginning and end of our lives on this earth will have dates, but how will we choose to live out our dash? For the follower of Jesus, that dash represents a life lived for the glory of God.

I'll go ahead and explain with a story. One day I was blessed enough to attend a Cincinnati Reds and St. Louis Cardinals baseball game with some friends. The seats were excellent. We were about ten rows behind the visitor's dugout where the Cardinals had taken up residence. My Pastor, Mark McMinn, was a huge St. Louis Cardinals fan. As we sat throughout the game, my attention was not drawn to the field or the players alone. Yes, the field was beautiful, the day was perfect, and the hot dogs were everything you would expect at a ball field for professional athletes. The outfield held a giant screen filled with statistics, updates, and commercials. Music was played, and mascots were on the field to entertain me between innings. Still, as nice as all these things were, none impacted my soul.

What do you think was fluttering between first base and second base? Yes, it was a beautiful monarch butterfly. Everyone in the stands was probably oblivious to it, yet I could not take my eyes off it. This winged insect brought more entertainment than anything requiring money that day. As the game progressed, it fluttered all over the field as the wind carried it. At times it was right near the first baseman Albert Pujols' head. Albert was well known, a homerun hitter and an All-Star. I found myself asking the little insect if it even knew who it was flying near. It fluttered again toward second base, where a line drive was hit. It appeared to be close to hitting my little friend. Again, I had an internal conversation with it to get off the field, or it would get hit. Without considering its safety, it flew through the path of the pitcher's throwing lane. I knew it could not survive the impact of a ninety-eight-mile-per-hour fastball. Thankfully, it timed its crossings safely, and the easily overlooked drama continued in clear view of everyone except without any play-by-play commentary. I saw it, and the revelation revealed to my heart was a subtle mercy from heaven for what felt like my observation only. Despite the environment, I could not take my eyes off this colorful little miracle.

I was in the middle of rebuking the butterfly in my thoughts again when the Lord spoke to me. "Why are you rebuking this butterfly? It's just declaring to everyone that it is a new creation. It wasn't too many days ago that it was just a worm with legs." It was here that I realized the spiritual, unseen chrysalis of salvation. That chrysalis of faith is signified by water baptism, where we are buried in Christ and raised to live as a new creation. The old life is dead and buried. What emerges is a new life, a new creation! Oh, I remember my time before emerging from the chrysalis salvation! I, indeed, was a "worm." Yet, God has transformed my life. Knowing this, I should live out my days like this little butterfly. As a new creation in Christ, I should not be concerned about the glory of this life, but instead, I should spend my life in glory to my Father.

This life has a chrysalis at the beginning and end, but I must not ignore the chrysalis of salvation in the middle. It is here that the Father transforms us, bringing us forth as a new creation in Christ Jesus. And what must we do? We flutter through life, allowing the wind of the Holy Spirit to direct us where to go. At times we awkwardly obey the simple task of expressing the transformation He has done in us in front of others. We carry the message of Jesus wherever we go. If the place is one of danger, where we will be facing the "fastballs" and "line drives" of life, so be it. If we stand before tens of thousands of people and only one person in the stands hears our message, it will be worth it. If powerful people are oblivious to our existence and see us as a pest rather than a blessing, it doesn't change who we are today through Christ's power. We have been given the wings of the Spirit. Soar with the message of the Gospel and leave the rest to God.

Chapter Five

Bilingual

As I get older, sights, sounds, and smells act as a time machine. When I experience certain things with my senses, I am ushered immediately to another time and place in my mind. I believe it is a gift from God to have a vivid memory. When I first began my prayer walks around Covington, such a memory crept upon me as suddenly as an eager child waiting for a younger sibling around a dark corner. I charted my path with intentionality. I wanted to go through the city park, the courthouse, and the schools. Doing this would encompass a large part of our city and crucial praying points. I don't know that there is anywhere I have walked where I don't have childhood memories, whether good or bad. Sometimes I walk past the house my grandma and grandpa Woodrow lived. I have turned off Washington Street several times and walked down the alley beside the home. That house, front yard, and back yard hold so many unforgettable memories of my grandparents and holiday gatherings with my cousins. It always brings a smile and a sense of loss for a time and people I cannot return to.

One morning, as I walked and prayed beside the Elementary School on Eighth Street in Covington, the Father sent a vivid memory to me, which turned out to be a subtle mercy. The scripture says, *"In his heart, a man plans his course, but the LORD determines his steps" (Pr. 16:9 NIV)*. This is true of my prayer walk. While I was being intentional for our community, God was being intentional for me. He led me to a spot and stopped me, reminding me of the significant moment that had taken place there. No, it was not the spot on the playground where I had been dared to run through the swings as an obstacle course, only to take the outstretched legs of Emily in the side. Once I landed, it took me a few minutes to catch my breath again. Neither was it another time when I had the wind knocked out of me from falling off the top of a giant metal slide on the playground's east side. That smooth metal contraption designed for young thrill seekers was capable of frying meat on hot days. The memory given to me by the Lord was not of the time in fifth grade when I married Kara behind the bell at the southwest corner of the playground. Our friend, Keena, came prepared with a black robe to officiate the wedding. I don't know if I am currently a bigamist or not because Kara and I were never officially divorced.

The list of elementary school memories could go on, but this one stopped me in my tracks. Just outside the east doors of the school, the area that used to be known as the first and second-grade hallway, on that sidewalk, is where I willingly said my first curse word. The Lord reminded me of everything that had led up to that moment. My friend, who had used foul language early in life, had taunted me because I wouldn't say the same words as him. He had noticed my replacement words like "gosh" or "shoot" and told me just to say the real one; nothing would happen. He spewed out a long train of words to prove that God wouldn't strike him down. I wanted to step back because he was not only fluent but eloquent in "trucker" and "sailor" talk. If lightning were going to strike, this would have indeed invited it! It didn't, so after some persuasion and being filled with a desire to belong; I did it.

There I stood as an adult, but my mind flooded with the memories and emotions of that day. Nearly forty years later, I felt the emotion of that eight-year-old boy. My friend had told me that "nothing would happen," but something did happen. I felt a big change deep within me on that day. I had opened the door to a new life that my parents did not live and raised me to live above. From that moment on, I began to use foul language with the same precision a surgeon would use a scalpel to do his work. My words were cutting to others and me. I was quick to carve others up for a selfish laugh or to inflict pain. With each use of words that I knew were not pleasing to my parents or God, I felt a heavy conviction. I pressed on, determined to belong until I was comfortable with my newfound form of communication.

The Father knew what He was doing when He charted my prayer path. When I cross this spot of formerly degrading transgression, my heart turns toward the power of Christ's transformation. In that spot that changed me all those years ago, I pray that the Father would help me guard my tongue. I often pray, *"May the words of my mouth and the meditation of my heart be pleasing in your sight, O LORD"* *(Psalm 19:14 NIV).* It took me a long time to reign in my tongue, and I still need much maintenance to keep it under control. God knows this by His omniscience, so He regularly brings it to my mind.

I meet with a group of men on Thursday mornings to pray. One day, near the end of our prayer time, the Lord gave me the thought, "Our Heavenly Father has no intention of raising bilingual children." That was it. Initially, I thought it to be odd. Bilingual children have some advantages in life. However, I knew God was not speaking to me of natural things. As I began to share with the men what I felt the Lord speak, more flowed from me.

How did we learn to speak? We sat in the presence of our parents. We looked at them. We saw their facial expressions. We listened and mimicked them. I remember watching my father and grandfather working on a car together. Both had their tongues hanging out of their mouths and grunted the same way as they turned wrenches. I laughed. I watched them walk side by side, and they walked the same way. I laughed. My grandfather used to tap his fingers on his chair as he visited with me. I caught my dad doing the same thing. I laughed. I see more of these traits in my life the older I get. I might as well laugh at myself. All of these things were learned by my father sitting in his father's presence, and they are the same things I have learned sitting in my father's presence.

We need to become like Jesus. Jesus said He would only speak what He has heard the Father speak and do what He has seen the Father do. How could He hear and see or know what to do except having been in His presence? Likewise, we must submerse ourselves in a baptism of the presence of our Heavenly Father. Once we set our hearts to pray, He will lead us to a place of personal revelation and transformation, just as He led me to the spot outside of the school. We must gaze upon His beauty in the Word, reading, praying, and waiting to discern His countenance toward us.

The Levitical blessing says that His face gives us His graciousness and peace! I can tell you that conversations with people who have grace and peace toward me are easy to listen to! How much more, our Heavenly Father? When we discern that He has a gracious and peaceful gaze toward us, we will tune in to Him often and receive all He has for us. Like an infant or toddler learning to walk and talk receives encouragement from their father, without fear, looking toward him as the one they seek to be fashioned after, so must we approach God with the same attitude. We walk toward Him and receive outstretched arms with a joy-filled welcome. We stumble and fall; He lifts us up. We weep, and He comforts us. We can come to this gracious Father and His presence at any moment to receive all we need.

It is in His presence that we hear Him speak to us. In His presence, we develop the prophetic ear and the prophetic tongue. We have to be close enough to hear before we can speak. We must have heard and understood before we can try to put together a sentence. For example, a baby knows what a ball is and what it is used for long before He can ever say the word "ball" clearly. In the same way, we must allow the Spirit to bring us great revelations in our prayer closet, allowing Him to help us understand those revelations so that, at some point, we can carefully and cautiously speak what we have heard from Him. When we do this, we are learning to speak His language.

We are not to be bilingual children of God. We must not learn and speak our Father's and the world's languages together. I remember being a teenager and accidentally letting a curse word slip while riding in the car with my mother. I knew it was not the language of my home, but it was the language of my life outside the home. My worlds collided at that moment, and I received a stern correction. She told me it "slipped" while I was with her because it was probably being used regularly when she wasn't around. She wasn't wrong.

We need a stern correction in the church today because we have blended heaven's language with the world's language. I am not just talking about coarse joking or foul language. The enemy has easily deceived us as he did Adam and Eve. Too many have been misled to speak his language through lies and manipulation because it is such a prominent voice in this culture. The result is an adapted Gospel that has reached a status of comfort in a fallen world. This has been fueled by fear because we would rather be accepted by godless people than suffer for the truth. Out of embarrassment of who our Heavenly Father is, we have asked Him to let us out of the car a block away from our destination. We have disassociated His true voice from our everyday lives, becoming comfortable with the world and ashamed of the truth. Let us never think we ever "leave" His presence. No, we do not! If we live as though we have, we will grieve Him! I promise you; that His countenance of love will never change but will take on a new expression of discipline and rebuke. He will not tolerate bilingual children.

The world spoke one language until they were united in rebellion against God at the tower of Babel. God said, *"If as one people speaking the same language they have begun to do this, then nothing they plan to do will be impossible for them"* (Gen. 11:6 NIV). He confused them as a protective work of his mercy. It stopped their activity and saved them from absolute annihilation. When we look toward the day of Pentecost, the nations were brought back together. The Spirit opened the door for the apostles to reach the nations. They spoke the wonders of God in an unlearned tongue, then they left that place and changed the face of the Earth with the Gospel of Jesus Christ. Twelve apostles and over one hundred other men and women went forth speaking the same language, by the same Spirit, for the sake of one Gospel.

Today, unity will follow when the children of God sit in the presence of their Father once again, learning to say and do only what they have seen and heard Him say and do. God is no longer dividing but uniting in Christ. Consider the Mediator that Jesus is! He brings unity between sinful man and the Father by cleansing us of all unrighteousness. He even became a unifier for Herod and Pilate, who had once hated each other until they found a friendship in their hatred for Jesus! How much more unity can be found among believers in Christ when we all seek Him and speak the same language of love toward one another? Paul encouraged this in the Corinthian church, *"Now I plead with you, brethren, by the name of our Lord Jesus Christ, that you all speak the same thing, and that there be no divisions among you, but that you be perfectly joined together in the same mind and in the same judgment." (1 Cor. 1:10 NKJV).* Oh, how different the church in America would look if the people of God would stop, shut off the voices of the world around them, get in the presence of God and listen. We would hear the Father's voice, and all learn to speak clearly for Him.

In a natural sense, it takes a lot of effort and practice to learn another language. I have long wished I could speak Spanish, but I have not made an effort to do it. Some suggest that if I were submersed in a culture that only speaks Spanish, I would begin to learn more quickly. Here is the answer to our spiritual condition. We must submerse ourselves in the Word of God, in prayer, and surround ourselves with the people of God. When we change the culture in us and around us, that same culture will flow out of us. Father, purify our hearts so the overflowing sound is the sound of Heaven.

Chapter Six

The Water's Edge

I have always been fascinated with the water's edge. The wonders of a child's heart and the inspiration of dreamers are both easily stirred there. Many tales of pirates and seafaring adventure have been penned at the water's edge. Don't forget romance. What novel or movie hasn't included a sunset stroll on the beach or a quiet float on a glassy pond? The water's edge is a place of discovery, exploration, inspiration, and aspiration. Before any explorer set out to find far-off continents or sunken treasures, they started first with a dream at the water's edge. What might be hidden below the surface? What dangers and beauty lurk under those swells? What passage might this vast desert of another kind hold for me?

There was a creek located on my grandparents' property. A creek provides endless entertainment for a curious young boy on summer days. On the surface, you could find frogs and water skippers. Just below the surface was a world filled with even more life and various treasures. A new discovery was made with every stone turned. When used together, a fishing pole and a piece of bread could provide a porthole through which the hidden thing can be brought into close view for observation. The tiny fish hanging on the end of my ice fishing pole was not quite as big a feat as landing a prized marlin, but the wonder in my young heart knew nothing of marlins and was delighted with the tiny minnow dangling from my line. Besides, a little imagination can make it seem bigger than it is and, at the same time, convince you that the shadow of the fish waiting in the water below is even larger.

The possibilities prompted a quick bait and a hope-filled cast. This pathetic display would be a mockery to great anglers of the world, but it satisfied me on many summer days. I wasn't Captain Ahab, and my passionate hunt was not for Moby Dick, but it didn't matter to my heart. I was at the water's edge whether or not there was a catch. Efforts were made to constantly discover what was below the surface. Each morning the minnow trap would reveal the day's catch, and the Ball canning jar I had taken from my mom and placed in the creek facing upstream often housed a crawdad. Those memories are of simpler times and flood my heart with joy even to this day. The smell of the woods and the sound of trickling water act like a time machine and, in a flash, take me back. It wasn't enough to fish or trap. The water was constantly calling me.

Oh, how I loved the rain and what it would do to the tiny streams I was drawn to. Spring rains would always bring an abundance of runoff from the surrounding fields. The typically dry grassy waterways turned into streams, laying the tall grass over to serve as a carpeted floor to the newborn river. The ordinarily small streams would then turn into what seemed to be an equivalent of the Amazon river. No, it was nowhere close, but it had become broad and rushing as the rains caused it to far exceed its banks. Dad and I went to look at the creek after such a downpour. He stood beside the water and warned me about the dangers of an undertow. He knew my curiosity, so he educated me with a good dose of fear in hopes that I might respect this now roaring stream, or any stream for that matter. He was wise to teach me this lesson at the water's edge. It is a lesson I learned and have taught to my own children.

One day, my childhood friend Nick and I found where the flowing water had eaten away some ground. It was a crater about three feet deep, twelve feet long, and six feet wide. At the bottom was a trickling stream that ran into a field tile. There was no danger here as the stream was barely past the soles of our shoes. We schemed a plot at the water's edge to plug the field tile so that it would make a swimming hole for us. We worked with all our might using rocks, sticks, and anything we could find to plug up the opening. Ankle-deep water was about all we could accomplish. That's when we decided to plug it the best we could and wait for heavy rain. We left it, and a few days later, it rained.

It was late August or early September. We had been in school all day, and it had rained hard for a few hours. It was a "gully washer." The sun came out as we endured the forty-minute bus ride home. The excitement to see if our experiment had worked was almost more than we could stand. Did the dam hold? If it did, for how long? Would the water have drained out already? Did it even work at all? Nick got off the bus at my house since our stop was before his and closer to our destination. We took off down the road in our school clothes because the situation demanded an immediate response.

After running about one-quarter of a mile, we found it. Our beaver-like engineering had worked! What followed was a conversation filled with challenges and dares, and before long, we had both settled on the story that we "fell" into the creek. We jumped in together, played, and splashed around in our school clothes and shoes. Whatever trouble this wet and muddy decision might bring would be worth it. We had worked hard for this moment and would not risk letting the opportunity pass, no matter the cost.

Once we arrived home, we stuck to our unbelievable story. Seriously, how could both of us accidentally fall in? Our parents weren't fooled, but like fools, we acted as if we believed our tall tale. Our shoes were set out to dry as our clothes were thrown into the wash. It wasn't until many years later that Mom and Dad got the whole story, though they had surmised it long before.

My time at the water's edge isn't confined to creeks and homemade swimming holes. One week each winter, we visited my grandparents in Florida. We would spend one day at Clearwater Beach. A picture of me at about seven years old is somewhere in a box at my mom and dad's house. I am standing with a rubber shark in my hand. My eyes were squinting, and my skin was quickly burning from the sun. Like my venture to the swimming hole in my school clothes, my sisters and I would pay for this day, too, but the sun-induced pain would be worth spending the day by the water's edge.

Since those days, I have learned about the danger of swimming next to a tile that is drinking up the pressurized water above it. Thank you, Jesus, for not allowing that plug to break free, sucking one of us to the bottom. I have also learned the value of an umbrella and sunscreen while on the beach. I have had many subtle mercies spoken to me while I contemplated life next to the water. The ocean's depths still beckon me to deep places of discovery with the Lord. He sets the water's limits but also puts life in its depths to be discovered, calling us deeper.

As a pastor, I have discovered a new beauty at the water's edge. It is here where the moment of anticipation overwhelms the one of newfound faith and baptism. The family looks on with joy at their loved one's decision. They walk into the water fully clothed, and no one gets in trouble for it. You can see the nerves and anticipation as the one to be baptized steps into the water. They aren't overwhelmed by the wetness of the water but by the wonder of God's goodness and forgiveness. When it is their time to speak, tears roll down their faces reflecting their grateful hearts. When they go under that water and come up again, it is a celebration that turns everyone's hearts toward heaven. We join in the rejoicing of heaven, praising God for His mercy and grace. Praise happens at the water's edge because the story of Jesus has been told.

On one particular trip to the beach, God showed me a beautiful picture that depicts what I am sharing with you today. As I sat and watched the water, I saw something more beautiful than the waves and heard something more moving than their splash crashing against the shore. A mother had wheeled her adult disabled daughter to the water's edge. Often, when people see a parent responsible for raising and caring for a disabled child, the first response is to pity them. "Oh, that poor mother. I couldn't imagine having to care for a child when they were so dependent for their entire life." I didn't think that on this day. Instead, I thought, what a blessed daughter.

Her parents could have left her at home. It would have been easier just to come to enjoy the beach alone, but they loved her so much they couldn't bear the thought of leaving her behind. Instead of just blessing themselves, they blessed their daughter. She was blessed because they could have just given her a view of the ocean up on their balcony, but that wouldn't have been good enough. No, they took her to the water in a balloon tire wheelchair so she could get her toes wet. Still, this relentless mother would not rest. She had a small cup. I watched as she leaned down, filled it with water, and then repeatedly poured it over the child of her affection as her daughter responded with squeals of joy. The mom laughed, and the daughter laughed.

At that moment, her disability was gone. It was gone to the mother who joyfully blessed her daughter. It was gone for the daughter because it was as if the waves were crashing over her. Oh, but they *were* crashing over her! Waves of mercy! Waves of grace! Waves of love and compassion flowed over her in doses that would not drown her. And it wasn't just one dose! No! It was thirty, sixty, and even one hundred times as that faithful mother continued to pour that cold, salty goodness over her!

My mind went to myself. How many times have I been disabled by my sin and flesh-filled life? How many times has God not left me behind but instead, doing all the work, He assisted me to moments of blessing? How often has He clothed me with His love, mercy, and compassion? How many times has He poured the oil of anointing over me, that saltiness that sets me apart from the world around me? I am loved. I am seen. I am cared for. He has never left me behind, and there are many more things He will bring me to, but today, I relish this picture of God's love. Once again, wonder and inspiration have been found at the water's edge.

Today, I am nearly fifty years old, and I still love to sit and listen for the voice of God by the water's edge. Maybe He would press out a little further in a boat so that I could hear Him better. Perhaps He is just sitting with me by the sea. Maybe He will walk toward me on the waves during seasons of stormy seas and trials.

Jesus did so much ministry beside and upon the water, but baptism was the only ministry He did "in" the water. I wonder if He hasn't used the musing hearts of humankind at the water's edge to draw us to Himself. If so, think of His grace! He covered seventy-one percent of this earth with water so we could always find a place to be baptized in His love.

He has grace to pour over you today, and that grace far exceeds any amount of sin you may have compiled or ever will compile. It doesn't matter how spiritually disabled you may seem. You may stumble and fall often, but He is calling you to get back up! If He must, He will see that you make it to the water's edge with Him so He can pour His love over you again. The atmosphere is perfect. Seek Him, and you will find Him! Explore the depths of who He is! Create moments where you can dive deep into relationship with Him! He is always ready to meet you at the water's edge.

Chapter Seven

People Watchin'

I don't remember how old I was when I discovered the joy of what April's grandfather called "people watchin'." People watchers could always be found in the prime real estate located at the center of the local shopping mall. These gargantuan shopping labyrinths are quickly becoming a thing of the past, but when I was young, they were where the young and old would go shopping. You could find almost anything you wanted at the local mall. Well, almost everything. Grandpa "Squeak" could never find Grandma Pat, so he would sit at the edge of the food court in the center of the mall for what he called "people watchin'."

Anytime April and I were there on a Friday or Saturday night, he could be found long before Grandma could ever be discovered. We would have a quick conversation. The usual questions were asked and answered, along with "what's Grandma shopping for?" What followed was a smile, a quick shake of the head, a short list of things he knew about, and an understanding that there would probably be more that would surprise him later. We waved, said hello again, or showed him our newest find each time we passed the mall's center. He even watched our bags a time or two during the busy Christmas season so we could keep shopping without being weighed down with all of our purchases. He was consistent. Like an oak tree that has stood on the same corner for years, so was Grandpa "Squeak," almost always found rooted in his spot at the center of the shopping mall.

As a young man, I felt bad for him. As an older man, I understand. It wasn't a punishment but a choice. There was a greater pleasure in his observation than in shopping. He was watching and learning. Friends would stop and say hello, and he took joy in giving a stranger a nod of approval as they walked past. He was never bored because he was "people watchin'." This joy of observing people has settled into my soul. I may not sit in the middle of the mall, but my eyes always watch people.

Is it any wonder God's eyes and ears are always attentive toward us? People are God's most extraordinary creations in all their beauty and chaos. Yes, greater than the tallest mountain, the deepest sea, or anything found in this vast universe. Everything else in creation was said to be "good," but after God had made humankind, he said it was "very good." Each person is unique in every possible way. In a crowd or on a busy highway, we encounter thousands of people who have their own stories, victories, tragedies, and dreams. I have often wondered about people's stories. I have been moved in my soul by the elderly couple walking hand in hand, caring for one another all these years later. And who can keep from smiling when a young family is filled with the chatter, questions, and cries of children? God is revealed through this creation! We can see the reason for His grace and mercy if we watch closely. And if we listen closely to the direction of the Holy Spirit, He will communicate prophetically to us about His love for them and us. For this reason, I have found that when I am "people watchin'," God and I are tuned in together.

At the end of one vacation, April and I were waiting to board our flight home from Tampa. I observed a mother trying to appease her baby. He was whiny. Every person who has had a healthy child knows what I am talking about. The baby was simply trying to communicate his dissatisfaction. He was ignorant in the sense that he could not adequately communicate his feelings to his mother, who was far above him in intelligence. The best he could do was articulate a cry. The mother did everything she could. She fed him. She spoke to him. She walked with him. She held him close and bounced him. She performed all these tasks and more at my approving smile. I remember those days well enough to know what was happening in the confines of her emotions. Not wanting to be an annoyance to others, she worked to appease her baby boy until, all at once, he was asleep. She sat down in the seat, gently rocking him with a blended look of relief and exhaustion.

While in line to board, I looked over to see this precious family again. This time the boy was awake and gazing at his mother with eyes of joy, wonder, peace, and absolute satisfaction. Once again, he may not have been able to communicate his feelings with words adequately, but those eyes, those windows to his soul, revealed everything. This scene was designed and created by God as a subtle mercy to me. Those innocent little eyes looked back to their source with a new revelation, attitude, and understanding. The Father pointed it out to me and reminded me of the psalmist when he penned the words, *"when I awake, I am with you"* (Ps. 139:18 NIV).

At that moment, that young mother looked down at the child of her affection gazing back at her. She acknowledged him in only the way a mother could. I watched as she spoke gently, and a smile filled his face. Yes, it was not just a smile with his mouth but with his eyes, and a coo came forth from his lungs. Again, he could not adequately communicate his heart for his mother, but the expression said it all.

I imagine our lives to be like that impatient child, trying to muster up limited communication toward our unlimited God as He looks on with eyes of love and compassion. He hears our request and reacts to it in love. He holds us close. He nourishes us. He speaks to us. He walks with us, rocking us up and down, back and forth, until we are at rest. He hears our crying and whining all the days of our lives until finally, "when I awake, I am with you." Then and only then will the trials and pains of the previous days fall off as He wipes every tear from our eyes for good. At that moment, we will look longingly into the eyes of our Source, our Savior, for all eternity. I am sure I will still have no words when that day comes. If anything, I will need to speak with a face-down posture and a few words.

What might that gaze be like? I can be sure it will be pleasant for us and Him, the One who gave His life for that face-to-face moment. He will, with joy, welcome us into all the promises He has prepared for us, saying, *"Well done, good and faithful servant"* (Matt. 25:21 NKJV). It makes me think of the apostle Paul. He expressed that the *"suffering"* of this life will not compare with the coming *"glory"* of eternity. *(Rom. 8:18 NKJV).* Hold on to faith. Don't get caught up in the whining of this life, forgetting God is with you and leading you to Himself in fullness. He's the only one who can be with us and still lead us to Himself simultaneously. The journey to the fullness of God's love in His presence will no doubt involve some whining on our part, but for those who remain faithful, it will end in awe.

Yes, this lesson was hastily typed out as I boarded a plane. April looked over a couple of times to see what I was doing and then asked what I was doing. I told her to give me a minute, and then I would let her read it. She understands when God speaks, you record it. As I shared it with her, we both smiled, knowing that the presence of God had met us in a public place while others were unaware. Right there in the middle of the noise and chaos of an airport, God used strangers to teach us about Himself.

We are disciples of Christ! If this is true, and we know it is, we can expect Him to teach us as we encounter others! Jesus was probably "people watchin'" with anticipation every time the disciples followed Him to a new place. Jesus led them to places they would not ordinarily go to interact with people they would not ordinarily interact with so they would be prepared to love others as He does. Every person healed, delivered, touched, or fed held a lesson for these future apostles. The glory of Heaven was revealed to them through strangers. Jesus turned their eyes away from thrones and positions of power to those who needed to be served. He turned their ambitions away from themselves and their agendas to His agenda of loving people.

The Great Commandment and the Great Commission go hand in hand. Jesus said the law could be summed up in two simple commandments. Jesus said, *"'You shall love the LORD your God with all your heart, with all your soul, and with all your mind. This is the first and great commandment. And the second is like it: You shall love your neighbor as yourself" (Matt. 22:37-39 NIV).* If we truly love God, we must love our neighbor. This is where the Great Commission comes in. As Jesus was about to ascend into Heaven, He said, *"Go therefore and make disciples of all the nations, baptizing them in the name of the Father and of the Son and the Holy Spirit, teaching them to observe all things that I have commanded you; and lo, I am with you always, even to the end of the age" (Matt. 28:19-20 NIV).* The Great

Commission was about people. If we love God, we will capture His heart for people. We will go to them and reveal His love to them. The love of God must overflow to compassion for our neighbors, even those neighbors we do not know, strangers whom God has brought across our paths to encounter Him through us! Will our eyes be open? Will we even see them?

I often wonder how many times Jesus walked past the lame beggar that had taken up residence outside the Gate Beautiful. He could be found there every day to ask for alms. Had Jesus not seen him, or did He know what was coming through his disciples?

Eventually, Jesus' training paid off. Peter and John noticed this man as they headed to the temple to pray. For whatever reason, on this day, they took notice and interacted with the man saying, *"Look at us." After the man looked at them, Peter said, "Silver or gold I do not have, but what I have I give you. In the name of Jesus Christ of Nazareth, walk" (Acts 3:6 NIV).* We know the rest of the story. The beauty of that moment could never have happened if the men of God had not been "people watchin'." If they had rushed to the temple to express their love for God, never noticing the opportunity to express the love of God to their neighbor, they would have missed a "God moment" that is still impacting lives today.

Keep your eyes on Jesus and the objects of His love – people. He will not only teach you about Himself, but He will also provide opportunities for you to participate in revealing Him to others. Who knows when a chance encounter will turn into someone walking, leaping, and praising God? Never be afraid to allow Jesus to lead you to places you would not ordinarily go to interact with people you would not ordinarily interact with because you will learn things you would not have otherwise known.

Chapter Eight

The Weight of a Scale

I stepped on the scale this morning. If you are anything like me, you know this statement will quickly spike fear in your heart. It was especially fearful this morning as I had not visited my old friend, the scale, for a long time. We have a love/hate relationship. I love that little device when things are trending in the right direction. When things are trending in the wrong direction, I tend to despise the scale and avoid it at all costs.

I have just come through a season of avoidance. Why did I avoid my little friend? It was not because I couldn't find it. It was right where it always was, next to the toilet in my bathroom. It hadn't become scarce in any way. I came face to face with it every morning and multiple times throughout the day, every day over the last several months, not giving it even a second of my time. Besides, I already knew what it was going to tell me.

The signs are obvious. My clothes are tighter, and my suits are snug. The mirror has expressed itself to me as well. My clothing and mirror have encouraged me to visit my old friend for months. Today is the day. Our visit was quick, lasting only a few seconds, but much was accomplished in that time. If only I could be as efficient as a pastor, filling my days with effective four-second counseling sessions that would bring about changed hearts and life transformations. One can dream, I suppose.

Why is it so hard to simply go to the scale and step on it? First, it is a truth-telling machine; I don't know that I would want it if it weren't. What good is it to have clothes and mirrors telling me the truth when my scale says something different? Scales do not have an opinion that caters to our feelings. They will not adjust the record of our weight based on our mood or potential response to its reading. If it did, it could not be trusted any more than my shifting emotions. No, scales are machines of truth. Even when we feel like it has lied to us, we measure it by trying another to see if it will be more kind.

Secondly, it doesn't beat around the bush or sugarcoat things. Sugar is what got me to where I am. The last thing I need is anything with more sugar! The blunt nature of the scale tells us the truth in a seemingly terse and inconsiderate way. Sometimes, the truth is heavier than our accumulated weight over time.

I have recognized a trend in my life. In seasons of irresponsibility, I tend to step away from the scale rather than on it. I do not want to have a confirmation of what I already know; my clothes and mirror have already told me the truth. The accountability of the scale, along with its seemingly quick and blunt nature, is the last thing I want, but it is the very thing I need.

Today, the scale is the third witness in my conviction. The clothes have testified against me. The mirror makes its declaration against me, and now I must hear from the scale. With a deep breath and a grimace, I stepped onto its creaking frame. It did its job with accuracy. It told me the truth, resulting in embarrassment, brokenness, and motivation.

Please don't feel bad for me. What I just described to you is true and necessary. Before I could repent of my lifestyle, I had to accept the truth and allow it to change me. As long as I avoided the scale, I avoided the truth and remained unchanged. Not only did I remain unchanged, but my busy lifestyle filled with fast food, unhealthy snacks, and emotional eating would bring greater problems than tight clothes if I didn't do something. Today, I came to grips with the reality of my condition, and I moved forward in truth.

There is a spiritual application here as well. Jesus said, *"If you abide in My word, you are My disciples indeed. And you shall know the truth and the truth shall make you free" (John 8:31-32 NKJV).* Jesus, knowing the hearts of man, warned against wandering away from the truth. He is, after all, *"The Truth" (John 14:6 NKJV).* Scripture is the *"Word of Truth" (2 Tim. 2:15 NKJV).* The Holy Spirit is called the *"Spirit of Truth" (John 15:26 NKJV).* Knowing this, we must make every effort to come to Him, focusing our hearts upon Him through the gathering of the body of Christ, reading the Word, and praying in the Spirit daily.

If we step away from the discipline of seeking Him, we can be sure our lifestyles will increasingly misrepresent Him to those around us. There will be outward witnesses that will reveal the condition of our hearts. Just as people can see how tight my suits are, so does the overflow of our hearts exit through our mouths for all to hear and discern. We can be sure anyone who is not regularly brought before the truth will live a life that sinks deeper into bondage.

I have seen this pattern many times. Someone will be in a moment of desperation created by bad decisions. They hear the truth of the Word, receive the love of Jesus, and encounter the presence of the Holy Spirit. Then, over time, they become scarce in church attendance. Usually, church attendance is the last thing in a person's spiritual life to go away. Often, they have left the Word and prayer behind long before they leave the gathering of believers. They progressively stepped away.

The Bible is a mirror of sorts. James says, *"For if anyone is a hearer of the word and not a doer, he is like a man observing his natural face in a mirror; for he observes himself, goes away, and immediately forgets what kind of man he was. But he who looks into the perfect law of liberty and continues in it, and is not a forgetful hearer but a doer of the work, this one will be blessed in what he does"* (Jas. 1:23-25 NKJV). When a person gives themselves over to sinful behaviors, they no longer appreciate the "mirror" of the Word. It shows us who we indeed are and calls us back to holiness. A person bent on doing things their own way will not appreciate the "living and active" nature of the Word. Hence, they avoid it, much like I have avoided looking at myself for too long in my own mirror. This only perpetuates our physical and moral decline. What is the adverse effect of avoiding the truth if the truth will set us free? Bondage! The Word will expose the chains we have taken back up, calling us out of them so that we may live free!

Once people avoid the Word and prayer, they will almost assuredly avoid attending church. The writer of Hebrews says, *"Let us not give up meeting together, as some are in the habit of doing, but let us encourage one another—and all the more as you see the Day approaching"* (Heb. 10:25 NIV). Why would someone avoid the gathering of the saints, especially knowing it was intended for their encouragement and edification?

Once again, I avoid the scale when I know what it will reveal about myself and my decisions. When we gather with others, we rub elbows with those of like precious faith. In a true church setting, there should be accountability for who we are called to be in Christ Jesus. It is a place where truth is spoken and holiness is encouraged. However, the one who has left behind the Word's authority and prayer has begun to step away from everything the gathering is intended to be. After some time, the church becomes like my clothes, restrictive and uncomfortable. These people often blame the church on the way out. I could blame my old clothes for their uncomfortable nature, but they haven't changed; I have. I could purchase new clothes a size or two bigger, but that doesn't deal with the real issue. If I change my clothing size without changing my eating habits, I will become more unhealthy and eventually need even bigger clothes. Likewise, a person who ignores their spiritual condition will become increasingly unhappy with the church until they leave it behind completely.

What about the church's blunt nature? Shouldn't it avoid confrontational messages to become more "seeker friendly?" Expecting a church to conform to your feelings and leaving the truth behind renders that church more useless than a scale that lies to us about our weight. At least a dishonest scale will have consequences limited to this life. However, a church that conforms, changing the truth to appease the emotions and feelings of people who have given themselves over to sin, is a church that harms people for eternity!

Paul warned Timothy of this when he said that in the last days, people will have *"a form of godliness but denying its power" (2 Tim. 3:5 NKJV)*. Any religion that worries about appeasing the emotions of godless people with a motive to keep them coming to their church services is a religion that denies the people the power that can set them free – the truth! So many people look at the church of Jesus Christ with the same disdain that I looked at my scale. They know they are sinners. The evidence is all around them. Why would they go to church and hear it put so plainly? They think to themselves, "Why would I want to go and hear what a bad person I am?"

Loved one, *"all have sinned and fallen short of the glory of God" (Rom. 3:23 NIV)*. All of us have had to come to grips with our carnal nature. Salvation is for everyone, so everyone must work out his own salvation. We must cry out to Him! Even after salvation, we must discipline ourselves to seek Him daily so that we might grow in grace.

I thank God for the Word, prayer, and body of Christ! I make it a daily routine to be brought before the Lord in prayer and study so that He can evaluate and discern my heart. On one particular morning, I was in prayer in the church basement when God allowed me to experience what it would be like to stand before Him. The room was dark. I was lying face down on the floor praying when He manifested Himself to me. I did not see Him because I was afraid to look up. For a few seconds, He looked into me. I know that sounds weird, but He did. The only way I can describe it is that my flesh was as glass before Him. There was nothing hidden from Him in any way. His vision had substance; I felt it enter me. As light is refracted in a prism, His sight separated and shot throughout my body. At the same time, He communicated with me by His vision, evaluating, correcting, and encouraging simultaneously. As humbling and overwhelming as it was, I felt the depth of His love for me. In those few seconds, there wasn't a part of my spirit, soul, or body that was left untouched. It was a unique experience I have not had since, but I know the subtle mercy of His truth when I seek Him each morning.

I pray that I am always readily available to come to Him for truth and be evaluated by Him. When I read the scripture, I pray that it speaks to me in a *"living and active"* way *(Heb. 4:12 NIV)*. I strive to ensure my prayer time is more than a list of petitions. My heart desires to converse with Him daily as I walk in the Spirit. I pray that every time I enter the gathering of believers that He uses them, along with the word being preached, to hold me accountable while molding me to be the man of God He has called me to be. I pray these things for you as well. Come to Jesus often! Let Him speak the truth in love to you, and be set free.

Chapter Nine

Priorities at Work

God created humankind with both the ability and the call to work. When Adam was placed in the Garden of Eden, it wasn't for a luxurious and lazy vacation. I have always told our church family that when the Bible says he was placed in the Garden to "work it," the Lord was not talking about dancing. Adam was given responsibility immediately after his creation. After his fall, the work that was once enjoyable now involved dealing with thorns, pricked fingers, hindered fruit, and labor. His work would now be by the sweat of his brow.

At that moment, the struggle became real. Fallen humanity, full of folly, tends to avoid work. We know this because we have a culture that is becoming increasingly lazy. Government handouts that were created with good intentions have now become counterproductive. Many have chosen to stay home and receive monthly checks, housing, and food assistance. I am not saying that those who are disabled or dealing with special circumstances shouldn't use these resources. They should. I have a very good friend who needs this assistance; it has been his lifeline. However, like any good thing, some want to take advantage of the system, choosing a path of slothfulness.

We need to take advantage of the opportunity to work rather than take advantage of others by not working. When we do, we receive more than a paycheck. Work is good for the mind and body. Labor can produce muscles that cannot be attained at the local gym, and it helps our minds stay sharp as we solve problems. Work will even help us socially as we learn how to build relationships with people from different generations and backgrounds of life. Work also allows us to engage the Great Commission and the Great Commandment. Spending forty hours a week with a group of people provides us with endless opportunities to reveal Christ to them and love them as He would have us love them. People have told me, "It must be nice being paid to do ministry." My response has been, "Aren't you being paid for ministry?" Our workplaces should be our mission fields.

I wish I could say I learned how to work early in life. Don't get me wrong; there were plenty of opportunities to work on the farm. Hay needed to be bailed and put away. Fences needed to be built. The yard needed to be mowed. Yet, I fought work at every turn. Part of the "folly" bound up in this child's heart was the folly of laziness. The rod of discipline was driving it far from me, but it would not give up without a fight. Thankfully, my mom and dad set an example of work ethics. They were both hard workers and would expect the same from us. When tasks were given, we were expected to finish them. Those moments planted seeds of understanding in us. When it was time to work, we were to do it until it was completed.

Those seeds were sown in me, but they didn't begin to produce fruit until I was a young man. It was a hard transition from boyhood to manhood. I went to work as a welder at WRIB Manufacturing for a man by the name of Larry Warrick. The Warrick family was known for their welding skills and hard work ethic. This was a rude awakening for me. I had learned some welding skills, but now I was learning how to work. Larry completed the destruction of the folly of laziness that was in me. I eventually embraced the value of a hard day of work and a job well done.

There are two sides to every fence, just like the ones that lined my dad's pasture. With work, there is the side of slothfulness and the side of becoming a workaholic. One must balance one's work ethic with an effort to avoid extremes. We must learn to rest without laziness and to work without obsession. God understood this when He established the Sabbath for Israel. While work has its benefits, a life lived at work without rest and worship is a life that will eventually break us down.

The pendulum swung the other way in me. Long gone was that lazy boy who was always anxiously waiting for quitting time and the weekend. I had begun to allow my work to define me. My self-worth was attached to my accomplishments at work. When I was a welder, I at least got to clock out every night and go home. Later, though, I was always on the clock when I went into ministry. I had quickly become a workaholic and wasn't aware. My condition became evident when I nearly had a nervous breakdown. This experience has driven me to inform young people who feel called into the ministry, "You punch the clock when you say yes to the call and punch out when you die." Ministry really can be a twenty-four-seven job. If you allow your self-worth and identity to be wrapped in what you do, more than who you are, it will burn you out. More than that, it has the power to destroy your marriage and harm your children.

I have made it a point to work very hard at balancing ministry and family. God has made clear in His Word that I cannot lead the church if I do not lead my family well. At no point would He call me to toss my family aside, driven by a worldly idea of ministry success. At the same time, He would not have me ignore my call to focus only on my family. I am called to both, and so both deserve my best effort. Ministry and family each have their moments of sacrifice. However, based on my workaholic past, there is always the potential for me to be so focused on the "work" of ministry that I could miss the opportunity to minister to my wife, children, and grandchildren. Because of this, I must know the balance between true priorities and what can wait, understanding what God has called me to in each moment.

This cannot be looked at from the standpoint of occupational ministry alone. Everyone must keep a balance in their priorities concerning their work and family relationships. Remember, the ability to work is a gift, but so is the ability to love and be loved within your family. Never throw one away for the other. You need both! Your work will provide for your family, and your family's needs will motivate you to work.

My aunt, Doris Jean Hall, was a great woman of God. I had to write "Doris Jean" because some knew her as "Doris" while my family always knew her as "Aunt Jean." She was my dad's oldest sister who exemplified the things I am sharing with you today. She was a woman of God and an intercessor. When I saw her at our family gatherings each year, she would grab my hand and say, "I'm praying for you and the church." I always thanked her, "because that church has a pretty messed up pastor." She would laugh and then encourage me to continue with confidence in the Lord. Ministry was her heart, which regularly overflowed toward anyone she interacted with. It wasn't done in a pushy way but with so much love, grace, and peace. You always walked away feeling blessed.

A subtle mercy came to me the day I officiated her funeral in late 2020. The service was lightly attended due to the COVID pandemic. Once it was over, we left for the cemetery in the funeral procession. The slow-rolling motorcade rivaled that of political dignitaries as we rolled past her workplace.

Aunt Jean had worked a long time at Allison Transmission in Indianapolis. I noticed something important as we rolled slowly by. They were hard at work, and no one noticed this precious lady who had given decades of her life for the success of that business. There weren't lines of people outside, and production wasn't stopped for 10 minutes to show honor. Don't get me wrong; I get it; that can't happen. However, the Holy Spirit pointed it out to me.

It made me think of another funeral procession. The family of an old farmer intentionally planned the funeral in the town of Attica so they could drive through the country, passing the farm on the way to the cemetery in Covington, about 20 miles away. While I must admit, it was a serene moment seeing the hearse in front of me with the body of the farmer pausing for a moment in front of the farm; the property wasn't aware. The crops someone else had planted didn't know the old farmer was passing by one last time either, even though the corn appeared to stand at attention on both sides of the road.

In the accounts of the old farmer and Aunt Jean, there was a line of respect, but it wasn't on the sides of the road where they had spent many hours of blood, sweat, and tears for their livelihood. No, the line was behind the hearse. The family followed closely because of their deep love and grief of great loss.

As I followed my Aunt Jean's body past Allison Transmission, the Holy Spirit impressed this thought upon my heart – "never sacrifice who follows you for the things you pass." Ponder that thought for a moment. It will encourage you to discern what is important in life. More than once, I have allowed my "livelihood" to cause me to sacrifice my "life." We must remember our workplaces won't follow us to our graves. Most likely, they will be too busy to even notice as our family rolls slowly by. Though we are to serve them well, our employers won't be putting a water-dipped sponge in our dry mouths hours before we pass. They won't change our soiled beds or make decisions for us when we cannot make them ourselves. No, it will be the ones who will weep over our passing. It will be the ones who will stay long with us, as Elisha stayed long with Elijah. The school of prophets was too busy, but Elisha loved Elijah and stayed until the last moment. So it is with our family and those who genuinely love us. We all must work for a living, but don't let the things you will one day pass become more important than the ones who will follow.

Chapter Ten

The Dynamic Symphony

When each summer was coming to a close and school was looming in the near future, a sense of seriousness would settle into my mind. For example, before I started the seventh grade, I made a pledge to myself and vocalized that pledge to my friend, Nick. I had purposed in my heart that things would be different this school year. In the past, I had gotten caught up in entertaining my classmates at the cost of my education and freedom. To me, there was nothing greater than getting a laugh, and I discovered I was pretty good at it. Not every teacher appreciated my humor or disruptive tendencies, so I spent time with various principals and in different levels of detention throughout my junior and senior high school days.

Some teachers had learned to appreciate my enthusiasm, reigning in my focus and redirecting me to something productive, while others wanted to draw lines in the sand to see if I would cross them. Unbeknownst to them, I loved a good challenge, so I accepted their invitation by crossing it often. The first group of teachers gained my respect, while the second group seemed to entice me to consequences that bore very little fruit. My mom tells stories about the times she would go in for teacher conferences, and different teachers would meet her at the door laughing. She would ask, "What did he do now?" Their response was, "He's not bad. He likes to have fun, but I can't allow it." It was a small victory to hear one teacher had said, "the problem is sometimes he gets me laughing too." As great as my moments of glory seemed to me, I knew I had to reign it in a bit, so that was my goal.

Every school year brought new possibilities, yet each produced the same results. I would be determined to be respectful, obedient, and studious with fewer disruptions. It really was in my heart, though probably anyone who knew thirteen-year-old me would doubt it. I admit my self-control stamina was limited. My commitment lasted about two days. I remember feeling like a failure, so I just didn't try anymore. I would ensure it was funny to everyone if it was funny to me. The problem with this mentality is that it ignores whatever else is happening at the moment.

One time, Mr. Field was standing at the blackboard teaching math, and I experienced a significant "fly kill" on my desk. The fly's guts were stuck to the desk's surface, rendering the little creature flightless. Its innards, acting as a chain would to a dog, yanked it back down every time it tried unsuccessfully to fly away. I learned that such a peculiar display of life and death was not more important than math or anything else that might have been happening in the front of the room. To try and draw attention to this special moment was inappropriate. The tone and focus of the room were on education, while my focus was on something else. A time of quiet detention, alone, during the first ten minutes of lunch, caused me to ponder the appropriateness of my invitation to "come and look." Let me pause here and say, yes, it was worth seeing, and that little fly gave me a lot of joy until he wasn't allowed to any longer. The issue was that I wasn't in class to find joy but to learn math. Today I am still better at laughing than I am with numbers.

Life has dynamics. Everything from conversations to church services has an ebb and flow to them. Life, like an orchestra, has its crescendos, diminuendos, and rests. In my immaturity, I had settled into one dynamic, fun. Because of this, I represented folly more than I ever wanted to. Humor has a time and a place. When applied appropriately to the moment's dynamic, it will end in a crescendo of laughter, bringing further joy and developing great memories that can be celebrated for years to come. When applied in a moment unfitting for laughter, it is counterproductive, inconsiderate, and obnoxious.

People of faith can do what I did as a child, selfishly settling for a preferred dynamic in the church. The Lord spoke this subtle mercy to me while pressure-washing my house, patio, and sidewalks. As I conversed with Him through prayer, He reminded me that He is recorded in scripture as expressing Himself in a whisper, by speaking, or with a shout. The people of God are found expressing themselves in the same way throughout the Word of God. He said to me, in that still, small voice, "The man or woman of God who chooses one of these three forms of communication as powerful and ignores the other two is a person who is following a flesh-centered, expected pattern of ministry rather than walking with the Spirit."

This was a powerful and liberating word to me because, as a pastor, there is pressure to meet people's expectations. Every week I stand in the pulpit, I am perceived in several different ways. To one, I am hyper-spiritual. To another, I am not spiritual enough. To another, I am too animated. To another, I need to show more enthusiasm. In the opinion of one, I share too much scripture, while others wish I would share less. I am overdressed to some, and others feel I should dress up more. The list of preferences is endless! The fact of the matter is this; I am not here to appease people even though I'm called to serve them. I am here to walk in the leading of the Holy Spirit in everything I do. In some seasons, there may be a shout that comes through me. In other seasons the Lord may be birthing a gentle message of His whisper. Still, another season may be filled with simple teaching with a speech that is very general in its tone. The power isn't found in the volume of the speaking. It is found in obedience to the message!

We must be careful to measure a message by something other than how quiet or loud it is. Measure the content with the Word of God. Don't measure the message's urgency by the volume it was conveyed. Measure it by the sobriety it brings to your heart and the action it stirs in your life. Some of the most life-changing moments I have experienced have come in the form of quiet conversations. Others have been through excellent teaching and, yes, even in the shout of worship. In all of these moments, I have experienced the power of Christ! As a pastor, I refuse to surrender to an "expected" pattern of what a preacher should sound like. Instead, I want to be the mouthpiece of God, having the freedom to speak as He leads me to speak in every season He brings me through. With Him, all forms of communication are powerful when Christ is at the center of it! Speak the Gospel boldly but let the Spirit set the volume. When we do that, it will be most effective!

This walk with Jesus is one of excellent dynamics. Without dynamics, music is either boring or obnoxious. So is the life of Christ to any believer who thinks God has one volume, one chord, one note, one key, or one style. I have settled into this prayer, "Father, let me know when it is time for a shout, a whisper, and time for silence." There are some things we address with a shout. Some things are best addressed with a whisper, and some warrant no response, so we remain silent. All can be done in the power of the Holy Spirit. We serve a dynamic and mighty God. I don't want to live by assumptions or reactive nature. I want to live in authority. I refuse to allow the enemy to dictate my mind or emotions. The Spirit within me has authority over those things and will dictate how they will react if I cooperate with Him.

He spoke to me again as I prayed about this very thing. I pray to our omniscient God regularly because my finite mind never knows what is coming for the day. He told me He is both the "Composer and Conductor of my life." Think of that! He is the Composer or Writer of my life. This majestic God I serve wrote my biography before I was born. This revelation settled into David's Spirit when he penned, *"All the days ordained for me were written in your book before one of them came to be" (Ps. 139 NIV).* Go back and read that entire Psalm so you can soak in the sovereignty and majesty of God! He knew us before we were formed in our mother's womb. He not only created us physically, but He composed our story! He wrote this day long before I was born. Every day fulfills what the Lord spoke prophetically about your life before you were formed. Like Mozart sat down at his piano and wrote symphonies or concertos, God wrote and ordained the days of your life. Ordained? Yes! Once those notes were on the page, they were ordained, established, and unmovable. They were placed within the correct scale, played in the correct octave, and at the proper time signature. There was to be no deviation from this.

Please think of the scriptures themselves. They are not to be added to or taken away from. When He wrote the Gospel narrative before time, though it had not been fully revealed to humankind, it was finished before it ever started. When time began, so did the metronome of His plan. When a symphony is written, there is no room for improvisation or selfish expression by any musician. The intent is that they follow what has been set in order by the composer, what has been written. God set the pattern that Mozart followed. He wrote it down before it was ever seen or heard by anyone. Before this day could be admired in any way, God admired it first, as He foreordained it. And it wasn't just ordained; there has been a volume and a pace set for this day as well. No composer has ever created a piece without a message attached to it. Today, there is a message, a revelation that the Father has preordained for you and others through you. Don't be like the juvenile version of me. My teachers had set a script for their day, and I had chosen to live by my own agenda. Chaos and confusion ensued. No doubt, my education suffered because of it. Yet, God, in His grace, brought me to where I am today. He composed this moment, and I want to be attentive to it.

We know God is the "Composer," but how is He the "Conductor" of our lives? He wrote the Gospel narrative, the lyrics if you will. He wrote the notes of my life, and I march through them to the time and tempo that He has set. However, I need to keep my eyes on what has been written and upon Christ, who is leading me. If we are to have any form of double vision, let it be such that we keep one eye on the written Word and another focused on His leading by the Holy Spirit.

The dynamics of music are written both on the sheet and will be directed by the expression and movement of the conductor. A good musician will see it in the music, see it in the conductor, and feel it within the song itself. Every day may have a new dynamic. It may be a "crescendo" of shouting. It may be a "diminuendo" of a whisper or even a "tacet" of silence, also known as a rest, or in a more Biblical term, a "selah" moment.

Each day has its own pace, one that God sets. I do not want to run ahead by assumption or fall behind in fear. Again, the music has a time signature, but the conductor will set that tempo. I never want to mess up the orchestra of God's love for others by assuming I can behave however I want in this season. It doesn't matter how well-intentioned I may be; if I ignore the dynamics of the love of Christ, I become a *"resounding gong or a clanging cymbal" (1 Cor. 13:1 NIV)*. By doing this, I would return to foolish adolescence in my thinking, acting on my own accord rather than following the lead of my Conductor. Since the time the Father spoke these words to me, I have made it a practice to ask for greater discernment. I want to be in tune and in time with what the Father is doing around me.

Keep your eyes on what has been written. Listen to the tempo of each moment and be sensitive to obey the leadership of the Holy Spirit for the changes. The end result will be a beautiful masterpiece. Discovering the joy in this journey can be challenging. As our days unfold, they bring with them emotions of joy and impatience. Sometimes He is unpredictable, placing a selah moment of silence when we think He should be screaming or roaring in power. Just remember God is in control. Even if today's music has become dark and filled with minor chords, know that He is with you, and the story isn't over yet. Calm yourself. Control yourself to stay within His will, and you will see the crescendo of His goodness on the horizon.

Chapter Eleven

Stripped of Pride

When I was young, I wanted to be a rock star. I knew I could do it because I had watched myself perform in the mirror many more times than I could count. The desire to be in front of people and perform has been a part of my nature for as long as I can remember. The passion for a life filled with the praise of men, ease, and wealth was a dream that was all too easily received. Sometime around 2001, the Lord began to stir my heart toward the call I had received at fourteen years of age. He began to write music through me, which was integrated into our worship services. There was no doubt that it was coming from the Lord, as He would often birth it during times of prayer. When our congregation embraced the songs, that old rock-and-roll dream started to spike in my flesh again.
My mind began to wonder if God had made an avenue within His Kingdom for me to get a little praise from others. Though it wasn't apparent to most, I was foolish and guilty of pride. Thankfully, God spared me from the desires of my heart by stripping them from me early and placing me further into HIs will.

God's reality is always better than our dream. In the beginning, I wanted to play my guitar in front of thousands on a stage of self-glory. I worked at learning the skills to play. Many nights were spent learning chords, scales, and riffs. I gained calluses and blisters but never the stage of glory or the thousands I dreamed about. The reality has been quite the opposite. This revelation came to me as I finished leading worship at the local nursing home. There weren't thousands there but thirteen. One precious lady always gets up and dances with me on the faster songs. On this day, she danced, then hugged and kissed me on the cheek, saying, "That was beautiful." The Lord endured my selfishness to allow me to attain just enough skill for a more glorious purpose of leading the few in worshiping Him. He has spent years breaking me down, moving my ideas from a place of selfishness to a place of humility. It hasn't always felt good, but it has always been necessary. That encounter, followed by a hug and a kiss, was more fulfilling than a thousand adoring fans because they came from my Father.

Many preachers have highlighted and dissected the disciple's arguments over who would be the greatest in the Kingdom of Heaven. We laughed at their ambition and sat with judging glares over their misguided focus. The truth is anyone with a call on their life must overcome the desire to be great in the Kingdom of Heaven and resist worldly standards of success in ministry. The apostles had given all to Jesus, followed Him in obedience, and saw an opportunity to the flesh. Were they in love with power? I don't know if they were in the beginning because there was no avenue to it. However, once there seems to be a path, it is easy to begin to dream of it until pride stirs up ambition. This was me. God began to use me for the Kingdom, and my focus shifted toward something else. The life of fame, wealth, and greatness, fueled by pride, had settled into my soul again. God would lovingly and patiently lead me to humble obedience.

Listen to what Jesus said to Saul of Tarsus as he was called to obedience on the road to Damascus, *"I will deliver you from the Jewish people, as well as from the Gentiles, to whom I now send you" (Ac. 26:17 NKJV).* Like Paul, we must be delivered from people before we can be effectively sent to them. If we are not delivered from their influence through humility, we cannot effectively lead them to Jesus. Following Jesus was never intended to be a life of ease. Paul's deliverance from people was a life filled with suffering at their hands. Paul would not be the only one to face suffering. Jesus told the disciples that they would face persecution and even death because of Him. This call is a far cry from the flesh-filled desires that often overtake our hearts. When we answer the call of ministry, we do not step into a life of comfort but a journey of obedience. There will be moments of trial and persecution, but these things are necessary for molding and shaping us into the image of Jesus. We must be delivered from the love of the praise of people, worldly success, and a life of luxury if we are going to become like Jesus.

When April and I took in our son, Kevin, as a foster child, I thought I would be the best dad ever. I felt like we had all the answers. A little love and discipline would soon fix his broken heart and behavioral issues. I was wrong. I quickly discovered that I was not as emotionally mature or equipped as I needed to be. He had come to us with many struggles from all he had endured in his first four years. The years that followed were not all bad, but there were many trials and disappointments for all of us. By God's grace, we grew through those struggles. I continue to tell everyone who will listen that I would not be who I am today without Kevin. His great need caused me to seek God like never before. Through him, God has taught me how to love sacrificially, developing empathy and compassion that would be distributed to broken families I would minister to years later. Kevin has been one of my greatest teachers.

Another time I was overly confident in my abilities was when I became the Senior Pastor of Covington First Assembly of God. In my pride, I thought I had it all figured out. I quickly discovered the weight of leading a congregation. The first five years held more pain than I thought I could bear. I knew people's lives were broken, but I had no idea how much pain it would bring. Sin is real and destructive. Death is unexpected and attacks all ages. Walking through grief with families privately while bearing the pressure of leading the congregation in public was a complex reality. There seemed to be pressure at every turn. At one point, I had panic attacks and thought I was dying. Add in another time in 2019 when I hit an emotional wall that almost took me out of ministry altogether, and you can see that the call to obey God does not guarantee a "rock star" life of fame and fortune. It does ensure us a life of fruitfulness despite the circumstances surrounding us. His plan for us exceeds the desires of our hearts.

Concerning these things, the Father spoke a subtle mercy to me while I worked from home. I was prepping myself for our congregation's natural and spiritual hunger. Their natural hunger would be met by the pork I had been smoking. At the same time, I was prepping my heart to receive and deliver the message the Father had prepared for their spiritual hunger. My location change meant I would have to change the location of my prayer walk. Although the Lord called me to walk the streets of Covington, He has seen fit to oblige my heart to be where it longs to be, in the grassy fields and wooded land behind my home. The morning had been a bit rainy but beautiful nonetheless. The storm did what it always does, bringing blessings in other ways. The ground was saturated with the necessary water. The sky had been set for a dramatic display. There was a gorgeous sunrise to the east, a magnificent rainbow to my west, the Word of God in my lap, and pork smoking its savory aroma beside me. Contentment would be an excellent word to describe how I felt that day.

On the previous day, the Holy Spirit pointed my attention to a corn cob stripped of its seed as I walked and prayed along the field. It was late September, so Autumn was approaching along with harvest. Initially, I saw it from the corner of my eye and kept walking. The next morning, as I sat in my moment of tranquility, the Spirit led me back to look at that stripped corn cob again. I obeyed, taking a walk to where it was. He did not call me to look at some ear of corn one hundred feet from my house. He hadn't shown me any other ear of corn the day before. There were undoubtedly thousands of ears out there, but there was only one He wanted me to return to. I knew my feet would be wet, and the walk was to the back side of the field, no short journey, but when the Father speaks, you obey.

I found the ear of corn in the field of corn. One would think it is like finding the needle in a haystack, but it was not. I knew exactly where it was. I could picture it in my mind, so I walked to the exact spot. The problem was that I had not spent time stopping and looking when He nudged me the first time. I observed this ear of corn like a crime scene detective. It was hanging upside down from the stalk with the drying husks peeled back as if someone had shucked it. The cob was bare. Not a kernel remained. The thief, a deer, had removed them with the precision of a brain surgeon.

My first thought was obvious. Here is an ear of corn, stripped of its seed by the enemy. There it hung, unable to be harvested for any good use and robbed of its value. My mind went to the scripture of the seed that had fallen on the hard path and how the birds had plucked it up before it could take root. Oh, how the enemy longs to steal the fruit of the Kingdom.

My next thought was of the organized church, not the bride of Christ. I almost always clarify that because people assume they are always the same. This empty cob could represent a church that has lost its posterity to the enemy. A church can be robbed of its next-generation when it establishes itself on the edge of the field. Tucked away a few rows into the field is a place of separation and safety from the scavengers who feast on those living on the edge. Safety is found in holiness. Those who compromise on trivial things and matters of holiness often walk close to the line, exposing themselves to danger. May we plant ourselves close to the center of the camp where the Spirit of God dwells and away from the edges where scavengers and robbers try to steal, kill and destroy what the Lord is doing. Many have embraced wicked things and planted themselves too close to the enemy's access. As true as this thought may be, it was not the only lesson the Father would teach me at the edge of the field.

The greatest lesson I learned from this empty corn cob was coming. It flooded my soul with hope. I am reminded that what the enemy meant for harm, God can and will use for good. The Lord showed me that though this seemed to be a loss, it had a greater purpose. The deer that ate those kernels of corn could not completely digest them. The deer carried them away, but many of those kernels will be planted once consumed and excreted. And not only with they be planted, but they will be planted in fertilizer to help them grow.

Even as the enemy tried to consume the kernels, God used that act to spread the seed.

Think of His grace! Even in your darkest moment, the enemy cannot completely consume and destroy you! It may hurt, feel crushing, and be dark, but like Jonah, you will emerge changed. Like Daniel in the lion's den, you will emerge stronger. Like the three Hebrews in the fiery furnace, you will see that there was another with you in the fire all along. The church, every time it is persecuted, spreads! Every time the enemy tries to consume you and your family, you find yourself in well-fertilized soil growing even more fruit after a season. From a pastor's perspective, even when families leave your church, especially for the wrong reasons, God can plant them and grow them elsewhere. In the end, His Kingdom can be worked out for the glory of Christ.

Let's suppose those kernels of corn had feelings and could communicate their story to us. Would they be able to see the good in it? I doubt they could find light in the darkness of the deer's belly, and the thud of landing in excrement can't be a pleasurable experience. Would the kernels see this event as God's will? If they were like us, they probably would not. Most of these consuming experiences have left me confused, asking questions like, "Where is God? Why has He abandoned me? Does God hate me? Is He unhappy with me for some reason?" We almost always overlook that the reason the corn was stripped from its cob was not that it was diseased but that it was good. The deer had inspected it and chosen it for its goodness. I will not say that it is impossible to face difficulties due to sin. That is a reality! Sin will bring us difficulties and eventually destruction. I am not speaking to those who have rejected God. I am speaking to those who have remained connected to His vine, bearing fruit and experiencing the pain of persecution. It is easy to question God's affection toward us in these moments. What we need to remember, it is our goodness that invites persecution.

Job was a righteous man. The enemy's attack came after God asked Satan if he had considered His servant Job. Job had been described as a righteous man. His friends would suggest he was enduring this attack because he had sinned and God was unhappy with him. Job rejected that idea. He endured well and received twice as much as he had before in the end. The greater thing he received was a new level of righteousness. Job had discovered his pride and repented. The trial had stripped him of all he had and landed him in a place of new fertility.

Think of Jesus. He suffered persecution as someone who was purely righteous. He didn't need to be brought to any repentance as Job did. However, scripture makes clear that He did learn obedience through suffering. Why was He hated? It was not because He was a sinner but because He was both good and righteous. The suffering of Jesus brought forth a multiplication that was greater than anything the enemy could have ever imagined. This one act allowed Him to become the worthy sacrifice for all men at all times. His life, ministry, crucifixion, and resurrection all happened in a short period, but the influence of each spans eternity in all directions!

Jesus promised the disciples and us that we would face trials and persecution. If we truly follow Jesus and desire to be conformed to His image, we must trust that he is using even our trials to accomplish His will in us. There is no way around suffering, so we should not look for a way out. If we do, we will find ourselves in disobedience. Keep in step with the Holy Spirit through difficult moments. You will find He is using them to mold and shape us to be more like Jesus. He wants to take our goodness, test it and grow it. That is His will. I often wonder if the reason we have not seen persecution in the United States has less to do with protective governmental policies and more to do with our lack of goodness. Are we not yet pure enough to face the refinery of persecution? Would our persecution be justifiable to onlookers because they know our sin?

Father, help me not to judge things prematurely or from a worldly understanding. Please remind me of the times you used various trials to strip me of my pride so I can be planted in humility. Help me see all things for your glory, whether my life is a full corn cob of promise or a seemingly unfortunate cob of emptiness. Either way, You are on the throne, and I trust you.

Chapter Twelve

Worship in Wonder

O ur family attended church. There was no question about what we would be doing twice on Sunday and every Wednesday evening. When I was young, the sounds you heard in our home didn't reflect the spirit of the church we were heading to. I'm not suggesting the tone was angry or the words sinful; it was the kind of noise and chaos you would expect from a house with five children. Inevitably someone had borrowed another's blouse and hadn't given it back. The bathroom was full; the house smelled like a combination of aerosol-expelled hairspray and the smell of burnt hair from the curling irons. There was the constant sound of the clothes dryer door opening, then closing, followed by the tumble of whatever was just placed in the drum. My role as the youngest child and only boy was to lay around as long as possible, only to discover I couldn't find my dress pants, socks, or shoes. I hated dressing up for church, so I made it a weekly battle. It was a battle I seldom won.

I don't remember any organized breakfast being made. If we had a moment to make some toast or fix a bowl of cereal, that would suffice. Mom was too busy throwing in a roast or tending to some other delicacy for a post-church service lunch around the dining room table. Some friends of my sister, Carla, called us the "Waltons" when we ate Sunday dinner, and they weren't far off. Each Sunday morning, the conversation was the same. Dad was flying down a gravel road that made a massive cloud of dust in the dry months, and Mom would be asking the girls if they had turned off the curling irons. After all, we didn't want the house to burn down while we were gone.

Sunday evenings had their own kind of chaos. Someone would be asleep. Mom and Dad would look to see where and with whom another had run off. My resistance persisted, but it was because of Mutual of Omaha's "Wild Kingdom" this time. It and the "Wonderful World of Disney" would come on television about when we were supposed to leave for church. I remember bartering with Mom about whether I could take some toys, especially *Matchbox Cars*, with me. Sometimes she would let me, and other times she would not.

I didn't hate church. It just seemed like we were there all the time. When you're a "busy" boy with a big imagination, the church could leave you feeling caged in. Boredom would lead me into trouble. More than once, I was sent out to my mom and dad, kicked out of Children's Church or "Super Church," as they called it. There's nothing like walking the walk of shame with every eye staring at you, including Pastor Allen. I didn't hate God. I had heard these Bible stories before, and I was tired of being told to be quiet, sit still and listen. One time I heard someone mention that a church service was so good, "This must be what Heaven is like." I remember thinking to myself, "what?" I didn't want to go to Hell, but I didn't want to sit in a church service for all of eternity, either! Praise God that person was wrong, and I didn't look too hard for a third option.

As I grew up, I worked out my own salvation. My faith was no longer the faith of my parents but a personal relationship with Jesus. I came to love the gathering of the church. This love blossomed into a season of personal revival for April and me. For three years, God stirred us. We did not know He was preparing us for occupational ministry, but He was. Eventually, I became the associate pastor of Covington First Assembly. After six years of ministering to our youth and leading the congregation in worship on Sundays, I became the senior pastor on August 1, 2010. Over the years, my love for Jesus has grown, but there have been times of dry seasons. I didn't resist going to church like I did when I was a child, but I had lost some of the wonder I had once felt.

In 2018 and some of 2019, I hit a wall. My emotions were raw; I was easily offended and started asking God to remove His call from my life. I had never felt this way before. I was praying and studying the Word of God consistently through that season, but I was facing great discouragement. Still, God was speaking to me. I pressed on and popped out on the other side of the wall. Then came 2020! Thank you, Jesus, for not making me go through a season like that while in the middle of a pandemic! He had begun to restore some of the wonder to my soul, even though the world was facing difficult times.

April and I escaped to the Smoky Mountains for our annual getaway in July 2020. I hear the Father's voice clearly in the mountains and beside their rocky streams. However, on this day, He gave me a subtle mercy in the middle of the Christmas Store in Pigeon Forge, Tennessee. Visiting this store is a tradition for us. We walk through and look at the trees, lights, and decorations, usually buying nothing. On this day, I would receive something more valuable than money can buy.

I heard a little girl repeatedly yelling, "Wook, Mommy, wook." I turned another corner of commercialized beauty to find her in a stroller. She was probably three years old. She yelled again, "Wook, Mommy, wook! It's BWOOO," or "blue" for translation. Mommy simply pushed the stroller, smiled, and said, "Yes, sweetie, I see it," with controlled excitement. I squinted my eyes as much as possible so the family could see my smiling behind my surgical mask. While I squinted my eyes, I could see that the little girl's eyes were never going to meet mine as they were wide with wonder and darting excitedly from one colorful item to another. The only thing that was moving faster than her eyes was her mouth. She had outbursts of declarations at an ever-increasing volume. At times we were close to her, and other times we were far away, but all the time, we could hear her calling out to her mom and dad, "Wook!"

Mom and Dad looked and a few times shushed her a little, but mostly they reinforced her excitement with a simple, "Yes, I see that," "Wow," and "Yes, isn't that pretty?" This little family was a joy to me, and every encounter I had with them made me squint my eyes to the fullest COVID mask-hidden smile I could. They sparked memories of my kids being small. For a moment, I found myself more enthralled with this little family than the lights and garland around me. Of course! Shouldn't we be more amazed by what God has made than what man has created? In this room designed to stir wonder, my wonder was stirred by this little girl's enthusiasm and the joy of her parents.

Then it happened. The Holy Spirit told me to look and listen again because He was trying to teach me something. He specifically told me to listen to what had caught my attention. It was the wonder of a child. It was the reckless abandon with which that wonder flowed off her lips. It was the joy of declaring to her mother and father things they already knew. It was the reality that they had brought her here for this moment, that they orchestrated this moment to spike wonder in their daughter.

How do I know? They weren't pushing a cart. They weren't there picking up precious items to purchase. Instead, they were bringing their precious gift into that place to spike wonder in her soul, to hear her cry out to them, declaring what she was seeing. They could see it and probably had seen it before, but they wanted to see her experience that moment with them!

What is my point? *"Out of the mouths of children and infants you have ordained praise" (Ps. 8:2 NIV).* That childlike faith allows us to trust and be born again, and that same unrestrained, fresh revelation brings forth anointed praise. God doesn't need us to declare things to Him so that He will know about them. Do you really think you can inform our omniscient God of anything? If you could, He is no God at all and unworthy of praise. Praise God; He knows all things! He has brought us here for this time, this season, to declare back to Him what we see. I believe Adam, being led through the Garden by God, and given the task of naming the animals with wonder, was a blessing to God. Imagine seeing those animals for the first time, declaring the beauty of each one back to God. If this is true of that moment, and I believe it is, so is it a blessing for God to hear our declaration of His wonders.

Wonder is found in new discoveries, revelations, places, and new experiences. For children, everything is new, and so everything is wondrous. One evening I caught lightning bugs with my grandchildren. I don't know why God created mosquitos, but I understand why He created lightning bugs, for the wonder of children, the thrill of the chase, and the admiration of the collection. I loved hearing them call for me to look at another insect. Though

I had seen them before, I said, "Wow, that one's beautiful," as if it didn't look like the last one or all the others buzzing around our heads in the darkness. It was special because it was their own. They had caught it themselves. And though this one looked just like the last one to me, they knew it was new to them.

Oh, may we never minimize the new discoveries of Jesus in the young! Let us always encourage their declaration and wonder by taking them to new places to discover new things in God! Remember that He has also scattered spiritual lightning bugs of wonder for us adults in this dark world. We must never let our knowledge or past experiences drive us to complacency. You may have caught them before, but have you caught one lately? At the very least, we can sit back and admire their beauty, or we could begin to catch and collect some.

God has new revelations for us every day. Every good teacher will bring forth new and old treasures. God is the God of both new revelation and reminding us of the revelations we have known. He does all of it to stir wonder and worship within us. Jesus had told the disciples that the Holy Spirit would "teach" them all things, "remind" them of everything He has said, and "show" them things to come. He teaches us what we do not know, reminds us of what we already know, and promises there's more coming! How wondrous is that? He has more for us today!

God restored some wonder to my soul that day in the Christmas Store. The culture of this world tries to drown it out because the news is always so negative and ugly, but God is calling us to rise above this world's downcast eyes and lift our gaze heavenward so that we might declare the wonders of His love to those around us once again.

Chapter Thirteen

Active Listening

I explained to my daughter, Alyssa, how a man's mind works. We can focus on something and shut off the sounds of the world around us, including our wife's voice. Yes, I have been guilty, and on this day, so was Garrett. There he sat, like a witness cross-examined on the witness stand while I did my best to help mediate his defense. He was guilty, just as I have been guilty many times. Admittedly, he heard her talking but didn't think she was talking to him.

She couldn't believe he was so engrossed in whatever was on television that he didn't even have the decency to listen to her talk to someone else. What followed was the subtle mercy of pre-marital counseling. Both were guilty. Garrett was guilty of not listening because he didn't feel it pertained to him. I chuckled as I saw him startled awake with the dreaded question, "Are you listening to me?" We all knew the answer. At the same time, Alyssa was guilty because she playfully snapped at him, not caring what mattered to him at that moment.

"He who answers a matter before he hears it, It is folly and shame to him" (Pr. 18:13 NKJV). James also commands us to *"be quick to listen, slow to speak, and slow to become angry" (Jas. 1:19 NIV).* This

is wisdom! So often, we attribute anger to a "quick" speaker, but that is not always the case. Of course, it can be attributed to the "angry" speaker, but it cannot be left there alone. Quick speakers are found in all kinds of emotional camps. "Humorous" fools laugh before they understand. "Arrogant" fools have a solution before hearing the problem. "Ambitious" fools give terse answers because they can't break their focus from their agenda long enough to hear. "Assuming" fools speak before they listen because their pride makes them think they have complete knowledge when they do not.

I have found myself in each of these places at one time or another. Many problems have been unnecessarily created because I was not patient enough to hear the entire situation. I have learned that "ignoring" leads to "ignorance" while "listening" leads to "learning." The ignorant person will speak out of their ignorance, while the listening person will speak from the knowledge and wisdom they have attained through the disciplined art of listening. Folly is found when we do not investigate and when we do not seek answers through deeper questions.

This investigation is called "active listening." The listener proves their engagement by consistent eye contact, social cues from facial expression and body position, and asking questions that encourage the other person to unpack the situation completely. Extended times of silence must follow our questions, so the other party has time to express themselves fully. One could say these things are: focus, expression, positioning, petitioning, and silence. This sounds a little like prayer, doesn't it? Is it possible that our natural relationships reflect our heavenly ones? Could our lack of listening and our ambition to speak "know it all" answers result from a prayer time reflecting the same mentality?

Too many times, I have acted as if I knew better than God. In my folly, I have approached His omniscience filled with pride, informing Him of what He should do. Folly has led me to make decisions in leadership through assumptions, acting without understanding matters thoroughly. These are things I am not proud of. I hope people have attributed these mistakes to my head more than my heart.

In our humanity, we are easily led to believe we are more significant than we truly are. To combat this, we must consider that our minds are limited and our understanding finite. We are not "all-knowing," so we must be careful to be "ever-learning." How do we do this?

We must focus our gaze on Jesus, not swerving to the left or right but looking straight ahead to Him. Prayer must be about Him more than it is about us. Prayer cannot be entered into with an attitude of doing God a favor by giving Him a few minutes of our time. This is the Creator of the universe and the Savior of our souls. He has invited us into His throne room, not the other way around. May we hold our tongues about ourselves for a moment and fix our eyes on Jesus! Yes, we are supposed to petition Him in prayer, but that is not all we are to do. Do you want to experience folly in a relationship? Find one friend and contact them only when you want something. I promise that the relationship will waver in its life-giving attributes. In the same way, we must approach prayer with a heart of worship, submission, and surrender as we remember what He has done for us. When we do, our prayer time will be full of life!

We must express ourselves before God. We are invited to *"Enter His gates with thanksgiving in our hearts, and enter His courts with praise" (Ps. 100:4 NKJV)*. That sounds like an invitation to connect expressively with our Heavenly Father! When the disciples asked Jesus how to pray, He started with "hallowing" the name of the Father. When we see a dear friend, we express ourselves. My childhood friend Nick and I don't even have to speak. Usually, when we see each other, we start laughing. I ran into him one day when his daughter asked her mom, "who is that man?" She answered, "That's Daddy's friend. They don't usually say much. They just laugh at each other." I have to admit; she was not wrong. What friend can ever greet another without an expression? When my grandkids see me, they usually yell, "Papaw," and come running for hugs. Oh, the joys of humble childhood. I know they must grow up, and maturity will change their expression someday. I'll enjoy this stage, but I will also love the next one. God wants us to walk into His presence with an expression too. Whether praise in a worship service or a sigh in the prayer closet, express your heart to your Father!

We must position ourselves in prayer. Some will say we should kneel; others will say we should stand; others will say we should lay prostrate before God. The body's position doesn't matter as much as the position of our hearts. Remember, we serve the God who spoke to Israel through Moses that Israel should *"circumcise"* their *"hearts"* *(De. 10:16 NIV)*. He wasn't as concerned with their anatomy as He was with what was hidden in their souls.

The physical work of circumcision was only done to teach about the internal work God desired in them. Men and women both have hearts or souls. Their lives need to be set apart. So when we approach the Father, our bodies should only reflect the position of our hearts. We are called to come boldly, but boldness does not equal arrogance. Humility is the posture with which we should approach our King. It is like a basketball player positioning himself under the basket. His eyes are upward, his arms are out, blocking everyone else out at the moment, and he is ready to receive the ball off the rim. Humility brings us low before Jesus. As we fix our eyes on him and block everything else out, we position ourselves to receive from Him. *"God resists the proud, but gives grace to the humble" (Jas. 4:6 NKJV)*. To be exalted is to have received grace from God.

We are invited to petition God, and so we must! I am sure you are grateful I finally made it here. I don't need to spend much time on this one because we get it; however, to allow you to hear the entire matter, I'll address it. God is not a magical genie. He is better than something so foolish. A genie, if one existed, would have no ability or desire to protect you from bad decisions. His role is only to grant wishes. If we had three wishes, we probably would end up with three horrible decisions, and the consequences multiplied three times. People have told me, "Be careful what you wish for." The same is true of petitions before God. We must be careful. I do not mean we must be careful in a fearful sort of way, but we should analyze the heart behind our petition. Is it self-centered, or am I genuinely trying to find the heart of God in this matter?

We often come to God with our solutions rather than hearing His heart. This is folly. Jesus spoke to the disciples telling them to ask anything, *"In My name" (John 14:13-14 NKJV)*. In other words, ask for things that align with His holiness and purpose on this earth, and you will see His hand at work. I have grown to ask for insight from God in difficult situations rather than demanding my way. In any quality conversation, two parties are speaking. Ask questions that invite answers and directives from Him. He desires to allow you to gain insight into the matter at hand.

Exercise the "nothing" of silence. Exercise and nothing are two words that fit nicely together when speaking of physical things, but we struggle with our tongues. Concerning prayer, I am convinced that one of the most challenging disciplines is exercising silence. Silence requires more self-control than we realize. It is not just about stopping our tongues, which is an astronomical feat. True silence requires focusing our mind, will, and emotions upon Jesus, remaining engaged with Him as we wait for Him to speak to our hearts.

Consider this, after hearing how Peter described the Holy Spirit had been poured out on the Gentiles; *"they became silent, and then they glorified God" (Ac. 11:18 NKJV).* In a moment when their religious upbringing had been challenged, they became silent, allowing the Holy Spirit to speak to and direct their hearts. Once there was an affirmation of what Peter had said, they glorified God. I have to believe this pattern of listening to man followed by silence as they listened to God was birthed after the pattern of their prayer lives. I also believe the erratic lifestyle of Christians can be directly attached to their erratic and inconsistent prayer lives. We rush into prayer, spew out a list of requests, and run about our days, thinking we have done something special. Is it any wonder we will not listen to others when we have never disciplined ourselves to listen in prayer?

Pastor Mark McMinn hired me as his associate pastor in 2004, but before that, I interviewed him when I was a church board member. During that interview, we asked him about his prayer life. While he expressed that it should not be limited to one hour, he used one hour as an example. He answered our question by saying, "In a sixty-minute time of prayer, there should be twenty minutes of praise, twenty minutes of petitioning, and twenty minutes of listening." You see, the time spent in praise helps focus our hearts as we express our gratitude to Him. A focused heart sees Jesus and can discern its motives, comparing them to His attributes. It is here that we can adequately petition and properly listen.

If you were to do a simple word search for "silent" in scripture, you would find it mainly used in a negative context. Jesus was silent before those who did not believe but demanded answers from Him. We also see where women were commanded to be silent in the gatherings of the churches in Corinth. However, when I speak of silence, I am not speaking of telling someone to "shut up" or withholding answers from anyone. Instead, I am speaking of meditation.

Meditation is nothing more than a silent pondering or musing of something. When I say meditation in church circles, some are offended, but their offense exposes their ignorance because they have either been misinformed or have ignored the truth. Yes, pagan religions have hijacked what God gave us and stolen what the ancients practiced regularly. Psalm 119 speaks of the significance of the Word of God. Time and again, King David talks about meditating upon the Law of God. David was a man after God's heart. This relationship was undoubtedly fueled by meditation, listening to the Father as he watched over Jesse's sheep. Today, however, the enemy seems to have taken this silent meditation, made it appear as though it were a bad thing, and accomplished his goal of shutting off our listening ears!

You may still need to be convinced to listen to the entire matter before speaking, so I will give you a little more clarity. Paul called it "praying without ceasing," but it is still the same thing David spoke of in Psalm 119 - meditation. We cast off praying without ceasing like it's an impossible feat when in reality, it isn't. Praying without ceasing is a heart continually contemplating and musing the things of God with its spiritual ear turned Heavenward! Those who meditate seek to hear the entire matter before speaking, keeping themselves from folly and shame.

A well-managed prayer life will result in a well-managed life that avoids the folly of speaking too quickly. Father, teach us how to pray, and while doing so, discipline us to listen carefully.

Chapter Fourteen

Gardening 101

Today I communed with the Father as I addressed the weed issue in my garden. I wasn't born with a green thumb, but I learned to grow tomatoes. My wife, April, loves fresh tomatoes with cottage cheese, and pots of chili on cold winter evenings always taste better with fresh tomato juice. Unfortunately, you cannot get delicious juice from weeds. Weeds, in fact, are the very enemy of the fruit I desire. In moments like these, I become full of pride and talk about my ancestors, Adam and Eve. Usually, I have a sarcastic "thanks a lot" for them as I try to pull these little life-sucking pests from the bases of my tomato plants. It's not fun, but it has to be done. If one wants a garden filled with a bountiful harvest, it has to be well-tended. It must have plenty of fertilizer, water, and the weeds have to be fought against with an effort that General Patton would be proud of. Yes, this is the ground we must take, and the weeds are our enemy! Over the top, men….I mean, Bob!

My first try at gardening came at a very early age. Our neighbor, Roy Rickets, always gave advice to me and my friend, Nick. The truth be known, he wanted us to find something to do on our property and leave him alone. One day during a visit, he said, "what you boys need is a garden. It will teach you responsibility." I'm assuming Roy hadn't noticed any real responsibility in our efforts to annoy him. If there was anything we were consistent at, it was finding some way to get him riled up. If we could have gotten paid for it, we would have been multimillionaires by the age of ten. However, we weren't getting wealthy, and Roy was right. We needed to learn responsibility and the joy of eating the harvest of our sweat.

I listened to Roy and planted a garden next to the playhouse in our backyard. The playhouse was a converted chicken coup, and my garden was a dirt spot that measured about three feet by five feet. I dug trenches with a stick and dropped in kernels I had gleaned from the corn crib. This was much more productive than what I would later do with that corn as a teenager, but that is a story for another time. It wasn't long before the corn began to sprout and grow rapidly. Some have said that it is possible to see corn growing in the humid Indiana temperatures, but I never sat still long enough to try. Nonetheless, it was shooting upward.

Then came the day I saw my dad cultivating his garden. The cultivator was a two-piece attachment for my dad's *Farmall "M"* tractor. One attachment hung from the underbelly of the tractor, and the other hung on the back. It had strategically placed spades that fit perfectly between the rows of corn and would dig up any weeds that had grown in the rows. He drove back and forth in the garden until the corn rows were cleaned out and the ground was softened to encourage better-established root systems.

Following this observation, I jumped on my John Deere pedal tractor and drove over my garden with less effective results than Dad. All that was left were corn stalks that better resemble toppled dominos than anything else. When I shared what I had done with Roy, he laughed as I had never seen him laugh before. Now that I think of it, it's the only time I remember seeing him laugh. Anyone who has planted a garden knows it is not a laughing matter when bad decisions, disease, insects, animals, or storm damage destroy it. It's disappointing. Time and money are wasted, but more significant than that, the potential harvest is gone.

I've come a long way since my days of driving pedal tractors. As Paul says, *"When I became a man I put childish ways behind me" (1 Cor. 13:11 NIV).* Knowing this, I exercised some of the responsibility that Roy had always hoped for and pulled some weeds. Gardens, after all, are places of responsibility. You can expect crop failure if they are not handled with diligence.

I will be honest. Right now, I am procrastinating. I prefer to tell stories of past garden successes. I could tell you about vegetables harvested, canned, juiced, eaten, and shared with others. However, I must get to the dreaded truth...I have a weed problem. Yes, the garden behind my house is only a reflection of my spiritual garden. What garden is that, you ask? It's the garden that is corrupted by my flesh. You understand we are all descendants of dirt, right? Adam was formed from the dust of the earth, which makes him "dirt" or, as God referred to Him, "very good" dirt. Adam was placed in the Garden of Eden for two reasons, to "work it" and to fellowship with God. Before his fall and the curse, I'm sure he would prune trees, tie up vines, and harvest fruit. The physical labor was enjoyable, just as his walks with the Lord in the cool of the day were bathed in sweet fellowship.

Then came the weeds. No, not natural ones like we see in our natural gardens, but the weeds of sin. We must acknowledge that the weeds found in the Garden of Eden and the garden behind my home are only a reflection, a visible representation of the weeds that sprouted in Adam's life the day he ate from the fruit of the Tree of Knowledge of Good and Evil. Yes, the first weed was allowed in Adam's spiritual garden, then the natural garden followed suit.

That first sin opened the door to a fallen nature that would produce sin without effort. I didn't plant or hope for the weeds in the garden behind my house, but they always show up uninvited. Likewise, weeds of sin were not planted in my spiritual garden by my parents or myself, but I sure have reaped a harvest of corruption throughout my lifetime. When I repent of one sin, pulling it up and casting it aside, another emerges somewhere else, secretly hidden among the good things in my life. It is deceptive because it looks so much like the good fruit-bearing parts of me, taking a similar shape of goodness, camouflaged until it has sunk its roots deep into my being. Before long, it has matured and multiplied. If it is allowed to mature, sin will create at least an embarrassing mess and, at worst, death. Tending my spiritual garden is a necessary and seemingly unending job. I exhaust myself at times with the pathetic things my flesh produces.

For this reason, we must be responsible and vigilant in that responsibility. This garden we live in, this fallen flesh, will produce sin quickly. None of us are exempt from the ability to produce weeds of sin. To turn a blind eye to our pet sins and accept a few spiritual weeds in our lives is to approach our garden with laziness. The writer of Proverbs witnessed a lazy man's garden, *"I went past the field of the sluggard, past the vineyard of the man who lacks judgment; thorns had come up everywhere, the ground was covered with weeds, and the stone wall was in ruins"* (Pr. 24:30-31 NIV). This man's natural garden had been overrun with weeds, and his wall was in ruins, allowing the clear vision of mocking neighbors, thieves, and animals to eat whatever fruit was left.

I desire to tend my spiritual garden with greater tenacity than my natural one. When sin appears, and it will, I must quickly pluck it out of my life with a repentance that will not be repented of. I must also keep the "stone wall" in place. I love that this passage calls it a "stone wall" because Jesus is the "Rock." This represents clearly set boundaries of holiness, a protective barrier built by Jesus within me. When I trip up and allow myself to tear down the standards God has set, I must quickly repair those boundaries firmly in my heart. If not, I can be sure that the enemy will continue to ravage my spiritual garden. I don't want to be a source of scorn and mocking. I do not want others to observe my life as untended, unprotected, and unfruitful. God help me to avoid spiritual lethargy and laziness.

As a pastor, I have learned that while I may see weeds in the spiritual gardens of others, I cannot weed their lives for them. No man can tend the garden of another. If he did, it would turn into trespassing rather quickly. I may see the weed, but until the other individual allows the Holy Spirit to bring light to it, pointing it out with Godly sorrow, it will not be repented of. My role as a pastor or friend is to cooperate with the Spirit of God in prophesying truth and encouraging others to aggressively deal with their own weeds. I can help identify them. I can teach them and give them hope in the Word of God. Ultimately, they must react to such truth by tending to themselves.

While I love people and pray adamantly for their various life situations, I must not become so engrossed in the spiritual gardens of others that I forget to tend to my own. When my focus is always on another, you can be sure my garden is being left untended. I cannot be so worried about the life of my neighbor that I forget to weed my own life. Jesus clarified that I must deal with the plank in my eye before I try to help my neighbor with the speck in his eye. A one-eyed weed seeker has no depth perception. Their vision is skewed, so they would do more damage than good if they tried the painstaking task of removing the speck from such a tender thing as an eye. To continually point out the weeds of sin in the lives of someone else while ignoring my own is hypocrisy. It won't be long before my unkempt spiritual garden cries out against my pride-filled judgment of others.

I will settle the matter here. There are a couple of gardens mentioned in scripture. First, the Garden of Eden was where God intended to walk with humankind. Yet, humankind chose to pursue something other than God, allowing sin to creep in. The other garden is Gethsemane, where Jesus agonized over the sin issue in humanity. In the first Garden, a man pursued disobedience while Jesus looked on. In the second Garden, men chose sloth in prayer as Jesus interceded for them. Three different times He asked them to *"Watch and pray so that you will not fall into temptation. The spirit is willing, but the body is weak" (Matt. 26:41 NIV)*. One could interpret the heart of Jesus' words as, "Disciples, a little slumber, a little sleep, and poverty will come upon you. As you rest, your field is growing weeds, and your stone walls are being torn down. Get up! Weed your garden, and get ready for what is coming!" They could not comprehend what He was calling them to at that moment. Adam had sinned because he was not communing with Jesus, and now the disciples chose sleep over prayer. If we are to walk in holiness, we must also commune with Jesus in prayer along the way.

The Holy Spirit is concerned with growing fruit in our lives so that He will bring light to the needs of our spiritual gardens. Tend them! Remove the weeds of sin quickly and pull them up, along with the root of pride that feeds them. Rejoice that God has granted you repentance but do not become prideful thinking you have arrived at a glorified state of holiness because you have not. Humbly seek Him daily; He will lead you to more profound repentance.

Chapter Fifteen

The Great Illusion

I am a sucker for a good magic trick. The art of misdirection and illusion has always intrigued me. There were moments of confusion for me, though. Magic was deemed evil by the church, yet a teenage boy, who would later become my youth pastor, used to come into our children's church and do lessons using magic. I remember him doing knot tricks with a rope and some classic card tricks. One time, he had a Bible that shot fire out when he opened it. I liked fire a little too much, so I wanted to know how that one was done. I asked him, but he refused to show me. Looking back, he took the "magician's oath" pretty seriously, refusing to let an inquisitive seven-year-old boy in on his tricks.

I would not be denied. I watched from across the room, waiting for him to set his Bible down. It happened! I fought the urge to run, even though the adrenaline pumping through my veins was screaming, "hurry!" I probably looked even more suspicious walking. My normal pace in church was at least a fast walk. Many times my parents or other random adults often corrected me to "walk, please." Sometimes the building took care of my much-needed correction as I bounced off the wooden columns that lined the sides of the sanctuary, each protruding about eighteen inches. The ominous "thud" could be heard throughout the building, followed by gasps and sighs as moms began looking to see if it was their kid this time.

Thankfully, there were no columns in the Fellowship Hall where this drama played out. However, I needed to speed up because I looked sneaky. At the same time, if I run too fast, he will see me going for it. Eventually, I made it to his Bible, removed the other books he had stacked on top of it, and opened it ever so gently. If fire shot out of it, everyone would know, and I would be in trouble. I tugged slightly only to find a hollowed-out box with a gadget that would strike a flint, causing a spark. I'm not sure what he used for fuel, but I at least knew regular Bibles were not natural fire hazards.

My confusion continues! Traditionally I find deception to be frustrating. I wouldn't say I like being lied to or manipulated. However, I don't get angry at the magician's deception. I would never invite someone to lie to me, but I would buy a ticket to watch a talented illusionist. Sometimes I can figure out how a trick is done, while other times, I cannot. My favorite is when the magician sets you up with something obvious, something you have seen before, only to amaze you by throwing a twist you never expected. I'm amazed each time, not in a man-worshipping way but by the skill and ability of the illusionist.

One particular morning I was walking and praying through the streets of Covington, and I noticed a tree that had suddenly developed buds. Not just any buds, but buds that will turn into flowers within the next week or so. I thought, "I guess this tree wasn't dead after all." There I stood in amazement at the annual winter illusion. The trick was almost over, Spring was near, and we were beginning to see that there had been life after all. Death would like us to think it has the final say, but it does not. It is only an illusion.

If someone who had never heard of winter investigated Indiana between November and March, they would be amazed why no one was crying out in fear and discouragement. Why is no one moved by the death surrounding them? They live in an area of cold, brown, and lifeless landscapes. The trees are bare. The fruit tree and even the nut-producing trees have long dropped their bounty. The ground has no life in it. There is no crop. No harvest. It is barren! Yet, people walk around peacefully because they know by experience what the newcomer has yet to learn. Winter is simply an illusion of death.

For example, trees do not die in the wintertime. Yes, they may give the appearance of death as their leaves begin to appear to dry up and fall to the ground. Long gone are the life-giving nutrients of photosynthesis. All that is left behind is a dry brown image of what it used to be. Its trunk and branches, once hidden, are now exposed as if they were emaciated from a long, challenging year of storms, drought, and frost. What would it be like if I could have a conversation with the fruit tree in the winter? Be careful approaching apple trees. *The Wizard of Oz* shows us the kind of attitudes they carry. Would I ask the apple tree and get a response? Would it not say to me, "No, I am neither dead nor dying! I am giving all my strength to my roots so I may grow taller this year and bear even more fruit than before." One might question the tree's comment, but soon buds will appear, flowers, leaves, and fruit. Then the illusion reveals itself, and we say, "I guess this tree wasn't dead after all."

We know this is true of the tree! Yet, we imagine we are dying when emotional "winters" hit us. When our spirits seem cold and dormant, we misunderstand what the Holy Spirit is doing in us. He calls us to put our roots down so we may grow and bear more fruit for the Kingdom. Just as the trees have their seasons, so do we. It seems the trials and difficulties of this life declare death to us. The emotional storms and droughts will take their toll until a season of "winter" finally hits us. Do you know what I mean? That time when it is dark and cold, and it seems the life has been choked out of you? Carefully rejoice if you have never lived through a "winter" season. These are not the great things we wish for as we serve the Lord, but they are necessary for us to be rooted firmly in the Rock. When the dark night of the soul comes, it is here that our foundations are tested, and the Spirit of God will stoke the burning embers in us, fanning the flame of our spirit to a full blaze again. It was in the wilderness where God intended to strengthen Israel's trust and resolve in His faithfulness. So it is with us until we finally see that we are alive after all.

A day is coming when life will spring forth again. We have seen this bit before! Like the magician's assistant disappearing and reappearing, we will already know what is coming when the curtain is pulled back, but it will still bring joy to our hearts. We look on with amazement at God and the mystery of His illusion. Our hearts race as we see the promise of a new day, warmth, beautiful colors, grass, and flowers. When we see the signs of this life again, we will declare what Paul declared about Eutychus, *"Do not trouble yourselves, for his life is in him" (Ac. 20:10 NKJV).* We will say what Jesus said to the young girl, *"Why make this commotion and weep? The child is not dead, but sleeping." (Mr. 5:39 NKJV).* Is it any wonder that Jesus rose from the dead in the Springtime? The angels spoke to the women at the tomb, saying, *"Why do you seek the living among the dead? He is not here, but is risen!" (Luke 24:5-6).* It was God who spoke to Moses at the burning bush and said, *"I am the God of your father — the God of Abraham, the God of Isaac, and the God of Jacob." (Ex. 3:6 NKJV)*. Later, Jesus referred to this statement as proof that He is not the God of the dead but the living! The patriarchs may have been physically dead, their remains returning to the earth, but death was only an illusion. They were not dead at all but very much alive in the presence of God!

We must quit seeing death as though it were more real than life itself. It's only an illusion. It is temporary. Like the illusionist's hand, it will play with our emotions, but the reality is this, we serve the God of eternal life. He sees bodies buried as though they were seeds planted with the intent of harvest. The individual is not dead! Their bodies are placed into the ground awaiting the end of the illusion, the final foe of death to be defeated. Just as sure as the dogwoods bloom in the Springtime, as sure as the tulip pokes through the ground every year, the dead will rise again. Jesus said some would rise to eternal life and some to eternal damnation. So, death is an illusion. Eternity is real.

You will exist for all of eternity. The question is, where will you exist for all of eternity? Jesus Christ came to call you to himself. Receive him and let death be nothing more than an illusion for you. Let it become nothing more than a curtain that reveals a passage to eternal fellowship with our Creator once removed. Receive Jesus and live!

Chapter Sixteen

Spiritual Immunity

While walking on my prayer walk, I was reminded that I needed to reorder my vitamin D3 supplement. Since the pandemic, I have been on a recommended regimen of vitamins C, D3, and Zinc. Studies have shown that these supplements, accompanied by a healthy diet, exercise, and sufficient rest, will help boost the immune system. During the COVID pandemic, there was much scrambling by pharmaceutical companies to find a cure. What resulted was multiple vaccines. These vaccines all bolstered their benefits and effectiveness. Before long, what was developed and advertised as a life-saving vaccine had become a competitive marketing campaign. Next, the government, highly invested in these companies, began to mandate nationwide vaccination. This wasn't a secret thing. The intention to make it very hard for unvaccinated people to live without the vaccine was publicly stated by our President. Then, certain states and cities imposed masks and vaccination mandates for state and city employees and those using public transportation or attending public gatherings.

Building up one's immunity was not the top story on the evening news throughout 2020 or 2021. Healthy diets, supplements, exercise, and sufficient sleep were rarely discussed. Even though no one said, "forget a balanced diet, exercise, and rest," it seemed as though we were good to eat whatever junk we wanted, sit on our couches, and stay up all night watching *Netflix* as long as we were vaccinated. Could we live a completely unhealthy lifestyle and be okay as long as we receive this shot? Of course not. No doctor anywhere would agree with this idea. I decided to make an effort to strengthen my immunity. In August of 2021, I began my vitamin regimen. I am not saying I will never be sick again, but I was not sick for almost exactly two years. Thank you, Jesus!

Before you judge me too harshly, please understand that I love and appreciate many advancements in modern medicine. When I was a boy, I had no problem faking sickness to get out of the things I didn't want to do. My parents knew this, so they set hard limits on what was sickness and what was not. "Do you have an upset stomach? Have you thrown up? No? You're fine! Did you say you don't feel good? You don't have a fever, so suck it up, buttercup."

My consistent fake sickness caught up with me when I was fifteen years old. I had been at Teen Camp for a week. While I was there, I developed severe abdominal pain. It was blamed on the sketchy camp food. When I came home, I still felt ill. I have never had stomach pain like this. My sister, Lora, assumed I was being dramatic, so she jumped on me and pressed my stomach. I screamed out in pain. My dad assumed I was faking and told me if I was sick to go to bed. I went to my room with visions of the boy who cried wolf.

In a mostly dark room, I prayed, "God, if I am supposed to die, take me, but if you have something for me to do, make someone believe me." After that prayer, my mom came in to check on me. Thank God for my mom! You could never question Mom's love for me or my sisters. She was and is always the one who investigates everything with loving eyes and ears. She entered my room and asked me questions as she pressed around on my stomach. In a few minutes, I was on my way to the hospital. Dad was arguing that it was a waste of time and money because they would send me back home. I don't judge my dad for this thought; I deserved it, and ninety-nine percent of the time, he was right.

It was quickly discovered that my appendix was severely inflamed, and they needed to perform an emergency appendectomy. My dad became quiet, and my mom was concerned. I was scared. It wasn't long before our pastor showed up to pray with me before the surgery. The doctors opened me up and discovered that the appendix had burst, but the poisonous infection had contained itself in a small area. In a few days, I would be able to go home.

I shared that story to clarify that I would not be here today without the combination of faith and skilled people in the medical field. It is not the minister's job to focus on a person's soul and discredit the doctor who focuses on the person's body. In the same way, doctors should not focus on the body and discredit the minister's role in the spiritual matters of people. The two are intended to work hand in hand for the entire wellness of a person. May we carry everything physical and spiritual to the Father in prayer that we might find wisdom. Concerning a person's physical wellness, that which is wisdom for me might not be wise for another. All our bodies are different, so each person must make their own medical decisions bathed in prayer.

The memory of my D3 needing refilled took me to another thought. What is the formula for developing a strong spiritual immunity? This question rolled through my mind as I turned north on Eighth Street.

If we are going to maintain healthy levels of vitamin D in our bodies, we need sunlight! We should expose our bare skin to the sun for up to thirty minutes daily. In that case, our bodies will produce a good supply of vitamin D. With a healthy diet, vitamin supplements, and some sunlight on my skin, my body will have a better shot at being healthy. Beyond this, do not neglect the disciplined balance of rest and exercise. If I can get at least seven hours of sleep each night and thirty minutes to an hour of cardiovascular exercise each day, my body will be healthier.

These realities led me to a spiritual formula. For a healthy spiritual immunity from sin, I recommend you have a healthy diet of the Word of God, daily exposure to the presence of the Holy Spirit, resting daily in prayer and meditation, and exercising faithful obedience to the Great Commandment as well as the Great Commission. I genuinely believe that if we do these things, our spiritual man or woman will be much better off. The temptation to sin may still be there, just as our bodies encounter natural viruses daily. You will encounter sin, but a well-equipped, well-trained spirit man or woman is ready to take on whatever they might encounter.

This formula is filled with spiritual disciplines. They require some effort. Spiritual health is not for the lazy person looking for "quick-fix" ideas that will save them time and effort. Are there "quick-fix" opportunities advertised in religious circles? Of course, there are. However, just as no pill or shot will make you healthy while you remain undisciplined in the natural areas of your life, neither is a life filled with religious "quick fixes" enough to sustain a person's spiritual wellness. Church attendance may have a benefit but is insufficient to bring about spiritual health on its own. For example, tithing once will not solve the debt created from years of undisciplined spending. One must discover the beauty and necessity of the spiritual disciplines in the formula mentioned above.

Consume the Word! *"All Scripture is God-breathed and is useful for teaching, rebuking, correcting, and training in righteousness, so that the man of God may be thoroughly equipped for every good work"* (2 Tim. 3:16-17 NIV). This is a healthy diet! The Word of God is full of useful, spiritual nutrients that will equip us thoroughly for every good work. If a person hasn't had the proper nutrients, their ability to work will be limited. People who live on sweets and processed foods may have bursts of energy here or there, but it will not give them the nutrients they need for sustained seasons of hard work. The trend with young people is to grab and consume an energy drink. It's a "quick fix" that does more harm than good. So many people treat their Bibles this way. If their Bible app reminds them to read a verse for the day, they feel they have gotten all they need. Inspiration may have been there, but they have not sought out the meat of the Word. They are still living on milk. Is there sustenance in milk? Yes, but God is calling us to maturity. We must get off the spiritual bottle and learn to feed ourselves the Word of God in its entirety.

Expose yourself to the radiance of the Holy Spirit. *"I say then: Walk in the Spirit, and you shall not fulfill the lust of the flesh"* (Gal. 5:16 NKJV). If you want to overcome the temptations of this life, walk in the Spirit. Remember, the disciples had their issues. They argued over who would be the greatest among them. Another time they asked Jesus for permission to call down fire from heaven onto a Samaritan village. They were far from perfect, but the Lord patiently walked with them for three years, exposing them to the power of God. Once they had seen the resurrected Savior and received the Baptism of the Holy Spirit on the Day of Pentecost, everything changed. Those who had once feared persecution now celebrated suffering for Christ. They no longer feared for their lives as almost all faced a martyr's death. They no longer sought to be the greatest in the Kingdom but followed Jesus' example of servanthood. They walked in the Spirit that was upon them. They lived in the power of God to not only work miracles but to live holy. There is no "quick fix" here. Just as exposure to the sun once every couple of weeks is insufficient for producing the necessary vitamin D our bodies need, so are sporadic encounters with the Holy Spirit insufficient for a consistently healthy spiritual life. So many Christians speak about what God did for them decades ago. He is the God of today, and so He has something for us today! His mercies are still new every morning! Each day is another opportunity to walk in the Spirit and overcome the enemy!

Rest in prayer. *"Watch and pray so that you will not fall into temptation. The spirit is willing, but the body is weak" (Matt. 26:41 NIV).* Jesus spoke of the power of prayer on the night of His betrayal. Peter, James, and John were charged to watch and pray. The result of disciplining themselves to obey would be a life that does not fall into temptation. We know what happened. They slept when they should have been praying. Jesus had already warned Peter that Satan had asked to *"sift"* him *"as wheat,"* but Jesus had prayed for him that his *"faith may not fail" (Luke 22:31-32 NIV).* Jesus had prayed for Peter, but now Peter was being called to pray for Peter so that he would not fall into temptation. I am grateful for Jesus' prayers! He is at the right hand of the Father, making intercession for us today, but we are also called to prayer. We have a responsibility in this thing too! Think of the Sabbath. God knew we needed a day of rest, so He made it a law.

Since the beginning, humankind has ignored the Sabbath principle and has paid dearly for it. Some believe that God should sustain them as long as they sacrifice their day of rest for the sake of the ministry. God may give us grace in seasons that genuinely are busy. Things happen out of our control, so He sustains us through those moments, but there are no promises to sustain a body that has been abused through irresponsibility. In the same way, we are to work cooperatively with His prayers over us by disciplining ourselves to pray so that we overcome temptation.

Exercise obedience. *"Since we live by the Spirit, let us keep in step with the Spirit" (Gal. 5:25 NIV).* The Holy Spirit has a greater work for us than simply avoiding the lusts of the flesh. There is work for us to do. Just as the thief is commanded to steal no longer but to do something productive with his hands, so must we do more than avoid sinful behaviors. We must become engaged in the work of the Kingdom.

Too many churches are filled with spiritually obese, lazy Christians. They gather around the table every Sunday, gobbling up the preached Word. They receive it with enthusiastic "amens" but seldom put it into action. God has called us to a kinetic faith! Just as the one who loves the table and all its delicacies but refuses to work will become physically unhealthy, so will the Christian who loves attending church but hates to serve will become spiritually unhealthy. There is no quick fix here.

There's no way around the Great Commandment or the Great Commission. We are called to do something. When our "doing" is more about "attending" than actively loving our brothers and sisters in Christ or going to love the lost, we have fallen in love with our Father's table, having never captured His heart. It is not only spiritually unhealthy to live this way but also leads to disobedience fueled by dead religion. According to James, *"Religion that God our Father accepts as pure and faultless is this: to look after orphans and widows in their distress and to keep oneself from being polluted by the world" (Jas. 1:27 NIV).* There is more to just avoiding the pollution of the world. The key is to spend your life working in the Father's harvest field. When we are busy with our Father's business, we will not have time to indulge in the mire of this world.

I cannot delegate everything to others. Some things are my responsibility and no one else's. My physical, emotional, or spiritual health cannot be entrusted to another. No one will eat for my physical health or become educated for my mental health, and no one will develop me spiritually. These disciplines are our responsibility. No one can force me into the sun for my physical health or reign my thoughts in for my emotional health, and no one can expose me to the presence of the Holy Spirit to attain strong spiritual health against my will. The same can be said about my prayer life and cooperation with what the Father has called me to do. All of these disciplines are ours to exercise and grow in. I pray that the Spirit is stirring you to become mature in these things. There is no other way, and you will never find a "quick fix" to replace them.

Chapter Seventeen

The Pacifier

It was lying face up like a dog playing dead at its master's request. The little plastic contraption was lying on the sidewalk, dirty and good for nothing but the trash can. I was about to cross Pearl Street toward the Elementary School when I realized what I had seen. It was a pacifier.

I sighed for a second because a lost pacifier usually means one of two things. First, a child is very unhappy, and an entire family is unhappy with them. A wise parent will check to ensure a spare pacifier is in their diaper bag before leaving the house. Ask any parent of a small child if they check the diaper bag for a pacifier more often than they check to see if the spare tire in their vehicle is aired up and ready to go. We already know the answer to that question. The chances of a flat tire are much more unlikely than a child crying uncontrollably in a public place. For this reason, April and I lovingly termed the pacifier a "plug."

The second reason to sigh while stepping over a dropped pacifier is that there's a chance the little one doesn't need it anymore. There is a slim possibility that it was dropped and forgotten. This thought leans a little more toward the subtle mercy the Father spoke to me about the pacifier. As I said before, I was about to cross the street toward the elementary school when I saw the pacifier lying on the ground. On this particular day, I finished my prayer walk later than usual. The first half was done as I walked to a meeting, and the second half was completed afterward. Because of this, children played at recess as I journeyed past the playground.

I love the sound of childhood. It doesn't seem like it was that long ago when I was playing on that same plot of ground. I can't walk past there without a smile. In this moment of reminiscing, the Father directed my attention to the children and asked me, "Which one do you think the pacifier belongs to?" I chuckled and answered plainly, "Hopefully, none of them!" He then dropped some things in my heart about the progression of maturity. Of course, the pacifier was on the other side of the street from the elementary school. That is where a pacifier belongs! The progression of maturity requires that we grow out of certain things so that we might grow into new things. We must let go of childish and immature things to grow into maturity.

I have attended many graduations and have never seen any graduates grab their diplomas with a pacifier in their mouths. Yes, the pacifier represents one hurdle in the life of maturity, but it is a hurdle of pole vault proportions for some kids to get past. After this obstacle, you can be sure there will be many more until they reach maturity. With every stage of advancement in life, there will always be a pacifier to leave behind. After a child learns to eat, the bottle must be left behind. After teeth are grown in, more solid food must be chewed. When a child can read, they should begin to read for themselves rather than being read to. Otherwise, they won't develop. What about marriage? *"Therefore a man shall leave his father and mother and be joined to his wife, and they shall become one flesh" (Gen. 2:24 NKJV).* Even in marriage, a young couple must let go of the pacifier of parental dependence so they can venture into maturity together.

The forward motion of maturity must always be present in the people of God. Paul spoke of spiritual maturity, saying, *"When I was a child, I spoke as a child, I understood as a child, I thought as a child; but when I became a man, I put away childish things (1 Cor. 13:11 NKJV).* Childish things must be left behind, like an unnecessary pacifier. Suppose you're going to cross over into spiritual maturity, into usability for the Kingdom of Heaven. In that case, you must leave your childish ways behind you and cooperate with the Holy Spirit until maturity begins to blossom.

We were designed to move forward. When I walked past that pacifier, I was moving forward. My motion was forward. My senses were forward, and the intention of my thoughts was forward. Think of the beauty of this reality! Your feet are designed to walk forward. Yes, you can walk backward but very uncomfortably. I remember seeing Michael Jackson do the "moonwalk" for the first time. I was about ten years old, and I wanted to know how in the world this guy could walk backward while looking like he was walking forward. Since then, I have seen too many people who can do this spiritually. Through deception, they appear to be walking forward in Christ, but in reality, they are backsliding into their sin and immaturity. Israel was guilty of this, so we must not allow our pride to lead us to believe that we are incapable of the same behavior.

Let us keep our senses forward. Our eyes were placed on the front of our faces for a reason. Our vision must always be forward-focused if we are to keep from stumbling. The same is true of our spiritual vision. We must keep Christ and His mission as our central focus. Otherwise, we will be like Israel in the wilderness, longing to return to our bondage.

The same is true of all our senses. Our ears, nose, and mouth are all forward facing. When we hear a noise behind us, we always turn to face it. When we smell something in the air, we turn to find where it is coming from, and when we taste something, it is with a forward posture. Even the sense of touch is best experienced with our forward-facing hands that reach out to feel things.

The work we do is always done in front of us. Stevie Ray Vaughn used to play his guitar behind his back at shows. It wasn't because it was the easiest or most efficient way to play but as an expression of his skill. I promise he played with his guitar in front of him in the studio. Progress has been established by men and women who have productive hands, moving society forward. The same could be said about ministry. Whether it is a ministry to our family or a community, the work must always be forward purposed. Even disciplining a child must be done with a future and hope in mind. In these things, we see our strength is forward-facing. Our spiritual strength comes from the Holy Spirit. He is always working the will of God in and through those who are yielded to His leading. By cooperating with Him, we can be sure that He will advance us in maturity so that He may advance the Kingdom through us.

What about our mouths? When we speak, shouldn't we be forward speaking? If you want someone to hear you, you do not turn your back to them when it's time to speak. I have often gently cupped my children's and grandchildren's faces to draw them close to mine, capturing their attention before saying something important to them. When God breathed into Adam, it was a face-to-face encounter. It was forward-thinking, life-giving, intentional, and eternal. And so this is how we must speak to others. Our mouths are intended to speak life rather than death.

I do not intend to be crude, but the only backward-facing part of our bodies is where we excrete waste. Yes, this, too, is key. Daily we leave behind us the things that are no longer useful, the refuse of yesterday's nourishment. We step forward to the new nourishment for today. For Paul, it was his accomplishments in Judaism. *"I count all things but loss for the excellency of the knowledge of Christ Jesus my Lord: for whom I have suffered the loss of all things, and do count them but dung, that I may win Christ" (Phil. 3:8 NKJV).* Before we can truly move forward to whom Christ has called us to be, we must leave behind our self-pacifying ideas and agendas to lay hold of the glory of the knowledge of God. We cannot pick up those old habits of sin any longer. We can never return to the life that once was. We must leave it behind, buried, or flushed away forever.

While our bodies are designed to be forward-moving, forward-perceiving, and forward-working, our minds should be forward-thinking. Now, this is not to say we should forget! No, the mind must remember where we have come from to stay focused on where we are going. It must remember the sting of sin. It must remember the past sin-filled failures and all that triggered such behavior. This is not done in a condemning way but for the sake of maturity. If the mind doesn't work properly, maturity will be stunted. The same is true of our spiritual understanding. We must never forget what God has taught us. Repentance will remember the godly sorrow that established it and will not turn back again to the previous life of sin!

Our physical bodies are designed to move forward, but they are also designed to grow up. My friend and former pastor, Mark McMinn, used to say, "Childhood is adorable, but perpetual childhood is deplorable." I promise you he is not wrong. There is little more disheartening than to see a man or woman who has all the potential in the world but refuses to become responsible. The level at which God uses us will be dictated by our willingness to step into spiritual maturity. A baby cannot drive a vehicle, and an adult who refuses to grow up into maturity may be big enough to drive a car, but they will never afford one due to their love for irresponsibility. The same is true of our spiritual maturity. We may physically grow, but as long as we remain immature in our approach toward God, we will be drastically limited in what we can do for the Kingdom of Heaven.

Let us not measure how tall we are alone. We should constantly measure our faith according to the Word of God. What condition is our heart in? What is the overflow of our mouths saying about us? We must mature physically and spiritually! Leave whatever pacifier you have been carrying and grow up! Anyone whom God has ever used has had to grow up to maturity. Isaac had to grow up, "So the child grew and was weaned" (Gen. 21:8 NIV). Moses grew into a man before leading Israel out of Egypt, "And the child grew" (Ex. 2:10 NKJV). Samson had to grow before he could become the Judge God had called him to be, "So the woman bore a son and called his name Samson; and the child grew, and the LORD blessed him." (Judg. 13:24 NKJV). Samuel grew, "And the child Samuel grew in stature, and in favor both with the LORD and men" (1 Sam. 2:26 NKJV). John the Baptizer grew up, "So the child grew and became strong in spirit, and was in the deserts till the day of his manifestation to Israel" (Luke 1:80 NKJV). Even Jesus had to grow, "And the Child grew and became *strong in spirit, filled with wisdom; and the grace of God was upon Him" (Luke 2:40 NKJV)*

Ponder these things today. I have only shared a taste of what the Lord has told me about this topic. There is more to be discovered, so seek Him for yourself. Ask the Father to help you evaluate your life. Pray through these forward-facing senses and ask if anything in you might be holding you back. I believe it is God's will for all of us to grow in favor with God and humankind, so whatever He reveals to you, repent and move forward in His grace.

Chapter Eighteen

Blessed Obscurity

If a tree fell in the middle of the forest and no one was there to hear it, would it make a sound? This philosophical question has been asked and discussed more than it needs to be. Of course, it makes a sound. What is sound but atmospheric waves stirred up by action? The only thing missing is the ear of someone to interpret those waves as sound. In other words, the sound is there, but the ear is not. If one desires to hear a tree falling in the forest, one must carry their ear to the place of the falling trees.

When I was a boy, I spent my summer days exploring and nights camping in the woods with my friends. The daytime is filled with noises. Birds are singing their songs and rustling the leaves of the trees as they flutter off wherever they think they need to be. Squirrels and rabbits scurry across the ground, and on occasion, you surprise a deer that had bedded down in the tall grass. The sights and sounds of the forest in the daytime are beautiful and unthreatening. However, when camping with my friends, beyond the gentle crackle of the campfire, the sounds become a bit more mysterious at night. We could hear coyotes yipping in the distance. Owls would hoot, and occasionally we would hear something cracking sticks as it walked nearby. In those moments, my friends and I would get quiet, investigating the mystery with a flashlight in one hand and a pocket knife in the other. We were sure it was something terrible. Too many ghost stories and horror films filled our minds. Was it a serial killer? Was it Bigfoot? Whatever it was, it held our attention for a few minutes before we returned to our conversation and laughter.

The forest is full of sights and sounds. Why would anyone place themselves among the timbers except to discover something not found in civilization? The fact of the matter is this; if one desires to hear or even see a tree fall in the forest, one must take the journey to discover it. They need to put on their hiking boots, grab their pack of supplies and head out to the wilderness.

Forests are for the few rather than the many. The opportunity to hear a tree fall in the forest doesn't come to the masses but the few. The masses will debate the possibilities, but the few will discover the truth and wonder of the moment. Think of it, while the world debates the philosophical question, an explorer prepares himself for the journey and then goes to experience it. He returns with a testimony of truth. His season of obscurity paid off and though others may tell him what he experienced wasn't real, he knew it was because he was there.

You had to be there. This statement has accompanied many humorous stories and even spiritual experiences. I have had my moments with both. It is difficult to articulate what really happened. Yes, I can explain it in the greatest detail, but until you are in that atmosphere, you do not know. You cannot smell the strange combination of aromas coming from the trees and plant life on the forest floor. You may hear about the tree crash but cannot comprehend the volume. You missed out on the sounds of the birds, bugs, and the crunching underfoot of leaves on the forest floor. You cannot comprehend the landscape change or how sunlight now shines on an area that has been shaded for one hundred years. You cannot comprehend its effect on the squirrel that had trusted the old tree and built its home high in its branches. You see, there is always more to the story than the sound. And so it is for all who will journey into obscurity to discover what few have seen or heard. You may return with a portion of the story to inspire others, but they miss out on the full experience.

Remember, anointings are received in the obscurity of the wilderness. Abraham, a sojourner, met with God on a journey and journeyed further with Him. Jacob was in obscurity when he saw a ladder reaching up to Heaven with angels ascending and descending on it. He was also in obscurity when he wrestled with the Lord. Moses was on the backside of the desert when he saw the burning bush and only returned to Egypt to bring his people back to that same mountain to worship the Lord. Samuel was just a boy hidden in the temple when the Lord spoke to him at night. David was watching his father's sheep when Samuel anointed him king, and then he returned to watching his father's sheep. John the baptizer lived in the wilderness and was a prophet. Even Jesus was so human that He was minimized by those who knew Him. From twelve to thirty, we know very little of His story. It was a season of obscurity where *"Jesus grew in wisdom and stature, and in favor with God and men" (Luke 2:52 NIV).* Have I given enough examples?

Men and women of God are not afraid to be found in positions of obscurity to discover what the masses can only dream about and debate. In a world of "talkers," the Kingdom of Heaven is filled with obscure "doers." Think of Peter, James, and John. They always went a little further with Jesus. They followed Him into a room where a young maiden lay dead so that they might see her resurrected. They went with Jesus to the mount of transfiguration to see what the others could not see. They went a little further to pray with Jesus. Had they stayed awake, they might have responded differently to His arrest and crucifixion. If they had remained alert that night, they might have also been able to see the angel that came to comfort Jesus in His time of need. What mighty things await those willing to journey to obscure places to receive invaluable experiences from the Father? It will only be revealed when we are willing to go places with Jesus that the masses refuse to go.

If the forest is always making sounds, we can be sure our Father is too. He wants to mold and shape us after the image of Jesus. We must choose to discover the obscurity of the prayer closet. We should prepare ourselves to shut the rest of the world out for a bit. When we do, and if we listen with our spiritual ears, we will discover that our Father has a Word for us. It may be a gentle breeze of comfort, still waters of peace, or the crash of discipline. Whatever it is, we know it is for our good, and we can reemerge with a testimony of His love. When we expose ourselves to the Light of Heaven in obscure places, maturity will be found there.

I have written of the end of a thing, but what about a beginning? There is something even more difficult to comprehend than a tree falling. What about fruit or a nut falling from a tree? The sound is far from a crash and more like a slight thud. One must be present and aware in order to hear and see the subtle reproduction of a tree. The nut falls and eventually takes root, becoming a sapling. This event is drawn out over a long period and would require a daily return to the spot to observe the little tree's progress. We know it happens because the evidence is all around the fallen tree. Hundreds of smaller trees which are direct descendants of the greater tree, now see their opportunity to thrive in the newfound sunlight. No longer shaded or obscured, they grow at an increased pace. Their trunks become thick, and their branches grow strong.

These are the seasons of those whom God calls. Seasons of obscurity followed by seasons of growth must precede positions of authority. A desire to be used by God must be balanced with a willingness to grow patiently in God. We hear His voice in the wilderness of obscurity and are tested in preparation for whatever He has called us to do. The ambitious seem to run untested, unproven into leadership positions only to be derailed by their immaturity. If you have a call into leadership, pursue that call carefully and prayerfully but do not despise serving in obscure places. Remember, Joshua would often stay in the tent of meeting when Moses would leave to address the people. There was no worldly ambition but only a passion for hearing the voice of God. He took his opportunity to grow under Moses' leadership until it was God's time for him to step forward. Joshua was a sapling, waiting patiently for God to bring him into the position He had promised.

In the same way, David was anointed king decades before he ever sat on the throne. There was much work that the Lord wanted to do in David before he became king. During that time, David never lifted a finger to advance himself but trusted the anointing God gave him through Samuel. God said he would be king, so he trusted the Lord to bring him into the kingship when he was ready. This allowed him to remain faithful while in obscurity and even as Saul pursued him. Though David had opportunities to cut Saul down, he waited for God to remove him. Once that tree had fallen, David rose up.

I also think of Matthias and Barsabas. Judas' spot among the twelve apostles needed to be filled, so these two names were brought forth as godly men who had been with them since the beginning. They had been faithful from the time John baptized Jesus until the moment they were called forward. A tree had fallen, and patient saplings were waiting for their opportunity. They were a part of the seventy that had been with Jesus and, at one point, had even been anointed to do ministry. As we read through the Gospels, these two men were in the background, unnamed, unseen, and quietly prepared for ministry. One would be an apostle. The other would remain somewhat obscure to humankind but beloved of the Father.

We never saw these two become ambitious. Their ambitions, if they had any, were hidden along with them throughout the Gospels. What feelings and emotions were they feeling in their time of waiting? What feelings or emotions did Barsabas feel when the lot fell to Matthias? I don't know for sure, but I can speculate that whatever they felt, it was reined in by the maturity they gained from spending three years in obscurity at the feet of Jesus. That maturity was solidified after they saw the miracles and the resurrected Savior. Though Mathias would receive the title of "apostle" by the casting of a lot, both would soon be baptized in the Holy Spirit on the day of Pentecost. They were both in the upper room, an obscure place that would be filled with the sights and sounds of Heaven. More importantly, it was a place where they would be filled with the Holy Spirit!

Do not be afraid of obscurity. If you feel overlooked and unheard by man, take your opportunity to seek the Father. It just might be a wilderness of preparation. Listen for His voice! Close yourself into your prayer closet. Root yourself deep into Him and patiently wait for whatever door He may open for you. Ambition is for the immature. They hate the humility of obscurity, but those who are seekers of Jesus love to go to places of obscurity where they might discover Him. We must be seekers of Jesus before ever seeking "positions" in any ministry structure. Regarding roles and titles, wait, learn, and grow with patience. Then, when the Father is ready to raise you up, step in with all humility and confidence that He will be with you.

Chapter Nineteen

A Shadow's Reach

I don't always consider the name of the street I'm walking on when the Father speaks a subtle mercy to me, but on this day, it was Liberty Street. It turned out to be a liberating moment for me, so Liberty Street was a fitting location. Mornings in mid-April have a slight chill. The harsh winter has been replaced by sunshine amid cool breezes, reminding me that a new season is approaching. The morning sun is low and blinding. Still, it is much higher at that time of day than it was in March.

The position of the sun in the sky is also a factor. It is in perfect line with the street, and there is no tree to obscure its radiance. These things and the fact that it was a cloudless day all played into this moment. I have to believe God's sovereignty knew I would be at this place for this time. He knew my heart and that my ears would be keenly tuned to His voice.

I had just carefully crossed Fifth Street with squinted eyes and my head down to help deflect the sun's intensity. That is when it happened. I walked over a tiny weed growing through the break line of an otherwise clean and well-kept sidewalk. At first, it meant nothing to me other than to say, "They missed one." However, God placed it there to capture my attention, not my opinion.

Covington is a beautiful little town with streets lined by immaculate trees. While their shade is embraced in the Summer and their leaves are spectacular in the Fall, their roots wreak havoc on the sidewalks. In certain areas, I walk on the edge of the street near the curb to keep from tripping or rolling an ankle. Liberty Street is different. Several years ago, the State widened it since it is a part of State Highway 136. They removed the trees, laid new sidewalks, put in new streetlamps, and planted some young trees. Because of this, the sidewalk is noticeably flatter and cleaner than most other sidewalks in town.

There it was, a tiny weed growing where it shouldn't. It wasn't a prominent place. Seriously, if the weed had been given a choice of where to grow, it would have indeed found a more fertile place than a tiny crack in the middle of a cement wasteland. Still, it was shooting forth, thin and with a few little leaves protruding from it. Its little branches stretched out on either side as if emulating the giant tulip tree nearby.

I didn't step on the weed, but I did step over it as these thoughts distracted me from my time with the Father. When I was about ten feet past the little green pest, the Holy Spirit spoke clearly to my heart, saying, "Go back and look at that weed. I want to show you something." I stopped dead in my tracks. I have learned to recognize my Father's voice and respond immediately to His leading. I walked back to the weed with a different purpose and perspective. My steps were slow as I kept my eye on the little green sprout. My focus shifted with my back to the sun, and my eyes no longer squinting. Long gone were the accusations of the weed's futile location or the homeowner's lack of effort to remove the ugly little pest. Now I was watching it to see what it had to say.

With each step, I realized that this little plant wasn't here by chance but as a testimony. It didn't remain because of laziness but because of intentionality. It wasn't futile or fruitless but would develop fruit in me if I could discern what the Lord would say to me through it. I can compare this moment to when my childhood home only had one landline telephone. The phone would ring, and all five of us kids would stop what we were doing to race to the phone in hopes of it being for us. This weed was a ringing phone, and I was on my way to answer its call.

Once I arrived at the weed's location, the Father spoke to my heart, "Remain small in your own eyes, and I will determine your reach." I didn't have to contemplate those words for long. He flooded my heart with multiple layers of explanations that would be meditated upon for the rest of my prayer walk and many more times since.

This weed was small, approximately two inches tall. The Sun was low on the horizon and brightly shining on its frail frame. To the west was the weed's shadow. That shadow was much longer than the weed was tall. To judge the weed by the size of its shadow, one would think it was several inches taller than it was. With a quick investigation, anyone could see the weed was small, but the Sun had determined its reach. Its shadow had far exceeded its actual size. At that moment, I looked up and saw my own shadow stretching far to the West. Judging by my shadow, one would suspect that I might be much taller than I really am. Suddenly the weed and I were alike.

God was calling me to understand the power of humility. I am to thrive wherever He plants me, remain humble in my own eyes, expose myself to the glory of His presence, and He will determine the reach or influence of my life. I don't need to project anything. I only need to remain in His presence. Like the sun would shine on that weed at different angles throughout the day, casting a long or short shadow in different directions, so will God use me in like manner. His glory is vital. There will be times when my influence is increased, like the low sun in the morning or the evening. There will be other times in the heat of the day when it seems there is no reach. The reach doesn't matter as much as the fact that I have planted myself in His presence!

This moment was so liberating to me because I have been plagued with an internal feeling of inferiority for most of my life. From a very early age, I have been afraid of failure. This fear has always pushed me toward a competitive mentality. Driven by an "I'll show them" determination, I have approached everything I have ever done with an attitude of proving everyone wrong and being the best.

I remember being about five years old when my dad hung a small basketball goal on the door in our living room. The living room was a gathering place for our family. My sisters got annoyed when I would come in with my Mickey Mouse ball and start shooting baskets. The ball would bounce everywhere. Sometimes they were gracious and would clap for me if I made it. Other times they would taunt me.

My sister, Carla, had friends named Rick and Jack. They loved to tease me. Rick knew when to stop, but Jack was relentless. One day they decided to challenge me to dunk the ball. I jumped over and over with all I had but could not reach the basket. The taunting turned to, "what's the matter with you? It's not that hard! Other people can do it!" I jumped off the chair repeatedly and still couldn't do it. Eventually, this dramatic and pathetic scene ended with me crying, followed by more taunting from them.

I was too small. I couldn't do it! In my mind, I was greater than my stature would allow me to be. This story is just one of many. Since then, I have spent my life in constant competition with myself and others, fueled by a root of pride. There is nothing wrong with success or doing your job with excellence. However, my striving was self-driven and self-glorifying.

I hated to lose games as a boy. After one hard-fought little league baseball game, I was in the back seat crying as my parents drove me home. I told them I was crying because I wanted them to be proud of me. My dad said something very sternly but clearly to me that day. It was such a powerful moment in my ten-year-old life that I could show you where it was said on Portland Arch Road. He tapped the brakes and looked into the mirror. He had adjusted it so he could see me as he spoke. He said, "You're my son, and you don't have to do anything to make me proud of you. I'm proud of you all the time." My mom reiterated her affirmation of that statement. The tears stopped that day, but I would not learn just yet.

My struggle to project an image of success continued. Driven by pride and a desire to receive praise from others, I threw myself into a frenzy of inward competition that would overflow into sinful behaviors and idolatry. When I picked up the guitar, I had visions of being a rock star and suddenly wanted to be better than everyone else, competing with the friends I had been learning with. As I played football, I was determined to be the best. I felt I had to be the best welder in my vocational class and in life. I wanted to be the best husband and father I could be. Even designing my home, I wanted it to be the best. Internally, there was this constant push to be the greatest as I secretly measured and compared myself to others. I didn't know it then, but a root of pride in me needed to be dealt with.

I wish I could say I left my ambitions when I entered the ministry. I didn't. There have been more ambitions in my life than I care to admit. I know I am in good company. The disciples needed to be corrected for wishing to be the greatest too. This pride has crept in at every level of ministry. As a youth pastor, I wanted to have the town's largest and most successful ministry. As a worship leader, I wanted our worship team to be better than any other church's. As a lead pastor, I desired spiritual growth in our congregation but was secretly excited about seeing numerical growth too. Numerical growth is, after all, the measuring rod of success in pastoral circles. If your congregation appears to be growing, you are celebrated, and I liked the praise of men a little too much.

That was a tough paragraph to write, but it is accurate, and this is my public confession. It's embarrassing to admit it, but I have repeatedly repented of this attitude, only to find it growing again sometime later. I am grateful that the Father is faithful to weed my spiritual garden daily of the pride that grows far too easily.

I learned a lesson about weeds and roots as a kid. When I was eleven, I got an opportunity to walk beans for a local farmer. This work consisted of waking up before sunrise, filling the biggest water jug you could find with ice water, grabbing a hoe, and heading to the farmer's house. We would pile into the bed of a pickup truck, and he would take us to the field. We would cover several rows each, depending on our age and ability. The objective was simple. If you see a weed, pull it, and do not leave the root.

My eyes were still crusted with sleep, and my hair was still matted to the side of my head. The sun was peaking over the horizon. The morning dew almost seemed like each plant was pouring a waterfall of moisture over my pants and into my shoes. It wasn't long before my shoes began squishing out the water they had drunk in. Then, my feet became heavy as the mud started adhering to my shoes' bottom and sides. My tracks had to resemble the imprint of a sasquatch. A quick swipe of the hoe across the bottom of my soles and I would be good for another distance until I had to stop and do it again. I learned early to appreciate the moisture of the early morning. While I wouldn't say I liked feeling wet at first, I knew the moisture would help as the morning progressed. The sun was coming up after all, and even though it was June, it would pour out a pretty intense heat for us. We would dry out soon enough.

Here, I learned the difference between various weeds and the best disposal methods. Some were tall and hard to pull like horseweed. Others were easy to pull, and still, others would vine themselves around the plant. The most important thing was to get the root. If the root remained, the weed would return. It would not only return, but it would also return bigger and stronger. Though the top of the plant was gone, the root remained alive, growing deeper and ready to sprout a new plant soon.

I suppose this is why people use statements like "get to the root of the problem." They know that if the obvious, sinful behaviors are visible in a person's life, there is also a root fueling that behavior. Cutting things from public view is not good enough; one must deal with the root. If the root isn't pulled up, whatever that issue is will return in full force and greater measure. We can be certain that behavior modification will fail us if we aren't willing to deal with the deeper issues of life. Thank God we have hope through Jesus Christ! We have hope of salvation, the root of sin being plucked up from our lives and cast into a sea of forgetfulness. Here was the root of my problem. Pride sprouted in every season of my life, and it will try again. I must remain planted in Jesus, rooted and grounded in Him. I cannot allow pride and ambition to drive my behavior. The message of the Gospel is too precious to be intermingled with selfish ambition.

For this reason, every minister of the Gospel must be consumed with making Jesus great. Beyond that mission, if I am to strive for anything, it must be to remain small in my own eyes and humble. It is not the call of God for me or any of us to be great by human standards or to rely on projecting a self-image wrapped up in material possessions or worldly success. Humble obedience is success in the Kingdom of Heaven. Take Peter's advice, *"'God opposes the proud but gives grace to the humble.' Humble yourselves, therefore, under God's mighty hand, that he may lift you up in due time"* (1 Pet. 5:5-6 NIV). Once we find humility, remain small in our own eyes, and stop trying to exalt ourselves, He will determine the reach of our influence.

Chapter Twenty

Swimming by Faith

W hen I felt the call of God on my life at the age of fourteen, I was initially flooded with emotion and excitement to serve. I was at Lake Placid Conference Center in Hartford City, Indiana. This has been a place of significance for my family. My grandparents took my dad to "Family Camp" there when he was a boy. He tells stories of the time he was woken out of bed by his mother, telling him his brother had received the baptism of the Holy Spirit. Dad, a little boy at the time, had spent his days all over those grounds. He swam in the lake and played all day, but now he was being pulled to the altar, unprepared by a worship service or a sermon, to receive the Holy Spirit. That night he received and spoke in tongues which the evangelist said sounded like a South African dialect. Anytime dad has visited those grounds, he still walks to that spot where he first encountered the Lord and begins to tear up. It's his "spot."

I didn't know it at the time, but God was giving me one of my own "spots" the night He called me into ministry. I stood in the back of that tabernacle, which was nothing more than an arched metal building with concrete floors. It looked like a metal airplane hangar filled with metal chairs. These "good ol' days" included no air conditioning or padded seating. Windows were propped open with two-by-fours all along either side of the building. It was dark outside, and the insects appreciated the lights in the cooler evening air. If the band wasn't playing, we could have heard the joyful sound of insects bouncing off the lights and window screens. There was a stage in the front where the Central Bible College worship team played music during altar time, just as they had the three previous nights.

As I looked up from praying, my attention turned to the guy playing the electric guitar. The Holy Spirit said to me almost audibly, "I'm going to do that with you." It was a surreal moment. Had I just heard from God? Of course, I did! I recognized the voice, and Bobby from four days ago would have never desired to do this. It was a call that I could receive. I loved music, even though I had never played an instrument. I could say "yes" to that call. Had He called me to preach at that moment, I probably would have said, "no, thank you." It didn't take long to realize I had some musical gifts. This was another subtle mercy from God. While it was a long journey through self-centeredness and pride, the Lord brought fulfillment to His promise.

Nearly twenty years later, I was a youth pastor, two years into occupational ministry, when I was asked if our youth worship team could lead worship for our Indiana District Kids Camp. Like that fourteen-year-old, I answered quickly with an adamant "yes." We went. As we were fasting and praying before our first service, I found myself walking through the "spot" where I had been called by God all those years before. He stopped me and told me to "look up." I did. Even though the old building was gone and the stage was facing a different direction, I knew where I was standing in relation to the old tabernacle. He spoke to me and said, "Today, I fulfill the promise I gave you as a teenager." It shot through me like electricity. At that moment, time had caught up with the preordained purpose of God for my life. We had terrific services that week and God moved mightily on those kids just as He had on my dad, myself, and my sisters.

The story can't be left here, even though there are more victories to share. At fourteen years of age, that stage looked like a glorious place to be. No doubt, the Lord used my pride and "center of attention" personality to nudge me toward the stage of ministry. Of course, He would not allow my pride to stay there, but in my immaturity, I desired to be the one rocking out on the guitar. He allowed that feeling for the moment, enduring my flesh to get the conversation started. The burden of ministry had evaded me in those initial moments. I was as ignorant of the troubles as the number of turtles I swam over in that green lake at the campgrounds. So, I must balance the testimony of God's victories with the warning that the call also brings some suffering. Don't you remember Jesus popping the disciple's pride bubble by telling them, *"All men will hate you because of me" (Luke 21:17 NIV)*? When you answer the call of God upon your life, you will experience blessings you never expected and pain you never imagined.

When Paul addressed the church in Corinth, he validated his apostleship because he had suffered more and worked much harder than the others. Too many see the ministry as an "easy job." I catch jokes from people about how preachers work one hour each week. I laugh and even make the same joke now. Too often, people in churches are unappreciative of their pastor because "He doesn't do nothin' but preach once a week." Thankfully, I am not in one of those churches! Sadly, far too often, lazy ministers have validated this thought of laziness. This line of thinking results in too many young people getting ministry degrees and approaching the "work" of ministry as a career opportunity rather than a calling. It seems like an easy gig, right? I'll admit I have a comfy chair in a climate-controlled office and often work with my feet kicked up on my desk (like right now). However, when "worked" properly, ministry can be a very fulfilling but challenging experience.

I'm not asking for sympathy. I want to be honest with anyone who feels the nudge of the Holy Spirit in their hearts to serve the Lord and His people in ministry. I have a warning for you if you are a young person who feels a call into ministry. No school, degree, or internship will fully prepare you for it. While they are good and necessary, they are as different as swimming in a pool and the ocean.

The Lord gave this analogy to me while I was on my prayer walk. Often you learn to swim in a safe pool environment, where things are clear, and you can touch the bottom if you need to. However, when you launch into your first ministry opportunity, you will find yourself in a deep, murky ocean filled with currents and waves of all sizes. Did I mention that they can all change in an instant? The water is wet, just like the teacher told you, but now it's salty and tossing you around. Not to mention, there are hidden dangers under these waters that weren't found in the safe water of your classroom or internship. You read about those things in books and heard about them in lectures, but now they are nipping at your toes, circling you with threats. Oh, how I remember the days of seeing things clearly before the waves got so big. I remember the easily navigated dreams and ideas I had in the pool, gaining the confidence to swim side to side with ease while believing that "when I get my chance, I'm going to accomplish so much."

Conversely, the vast ocean of ministry is exhausting. The distance for simple tasks is further away, and the boatload of programs you must drag along with you will slow you down. It's much harder to swim in the ocean than in a pool. When we receive the call, we respond with joy as if our friend asked us to go for a swim on a hot summer day. Yes, of course! Our quick answer is made from simple faith and obedience, unaware of the joys and troubles that lie ahead. That is why we don't swim for pleasure, but the adventure, for the challenge, and most importantly, because we have been called to do it. Remember, Jesus walked on the waves, He calmed the disciples every time they toiled, and He has the power to calm the wind and waves today. He'll even part the waters sometimes when we need a reprieve.

By faith! That's how we do it! By depending on the Holy Spirit for leading and strength through difficult times. Like Paul, we will face moments of suffering and a lot of hard work. Sometimes it will exasperate us, and we will feel like we are sinking, but He will never leave or forsake us! He will uphold us with His righteous right hand!

Before you launch yourself or someone else into ministry, remember that "hard work" must already be active in your or their life. If they are a "floater" or a "coaster" and approach life with no movement or momentum, they may survive, but they won't accomplish much. Find out what Jesus has called and equipped you to do because taking things on that He has not called you to do will drown you. Make sure you have been tested by enduring some suffering and hard work before you dive in but once you have been tested, jump into the next test because He will see you through it!

Press on with a Michael Phelps stride as you move forward in the things God has called you to, and never forget that there is a great cloud of witnesses cheering you on.

Chapter Twenty-One

Afterglow

F ire and water are natural enemies. Water, when placed on wood, will keep it from igniting. Water on a campfire will douse its energy. Water on a grease fire will spread it. However, there is a time when fire and water seem to work beautifully together. Oceanic sunsets are especially effective. It is here where water and fire are in perfect cohesion as they produce an awe-inspiring event that will always draw a crowd. Each time a burning sun touches a liquid horizon, amateur and professional photographers will gather at the water's edge to capture the moment. Young couples pose for a memorable photo, while aged couples greatly appreciate every past and present sunset they absorb.

I don't know anyone who appreciates a sunset more than my father, a picture of him exercising his evening ritual while on the beach is hanging on my office wall. I'm not speaking of some pagan indulgence. No, it's the admiration of the God-created and God-scheduled event that happens at a particular time each evening. The ritual begins about an hour before the actual sunset starts. A discussion is held about the time the sun will set on that particular day. There may be a plethora of activities happening, and dinner may be ready to eat, but everything else is secondary to the preordained agenda of the evening. Dad will head out with urgency to stand on the beach moments before the sun descends on the horizon. Though the sky is starting to darken, you can see his face light up with boyish wonder. When the first edge hits the water, he announces it and begins to time how quickly the entire ball of fire sinks beneath the water.

I learned something from him years ago. Once the sun drops below the horizon, take in the wonder of the fading orange to the west for a few minutes but be sure to turn around. If you're lucky enough to have a few clouds in the atmosphere of the eastern sky to reflect and refract the remaining light, you will see an explosion of color. This is the afterglow. It is the diminuendo of a day, fading out in beautiful tones that are as admirable as the setting sun itself. It is the swan song of a day well done, as remnants of it still dance across the sky in celebration. This afterglow is no more eternal than the sunset. It is temporal, for a moment, fading with promises of tomorrow's new day.

There is another time when fire and water come together to create an afterglow, and that is at the outpouring of the Holy Spirit. He is referred to as fire all through the Old Testament. He is that fire in the burning bush, the pillar of fire before Israel, and that glorious burning at the top of Mt. Sinai. The fire on the altar was a representation of His presence. We see in Acts Chapter Two where the Spirit was poured out, and tongues of fire settled into the heads of those who received.

That explains the fire, but what about the water? We, like the earth, are over seventy percent water. When the Holy Spirit is poured out on our lives, the Father creates an attractive intermingling of His creation and Glory. On that first outpouring at Pentecost, thousands were drawn to the sight and believed when they heard the message. The fire had intermingled with water, and the crowds gathered. The afterglow of that moment is still impacting the world today!

When Moses came from the presence of God, he walked with an afterglow of the glorious encounter. When the glory of God interacted with his face, it continued to reflect and refract the beauty of the Father. If this was the glory of such an encounter before the ascension of Jesus and the distribution of the Holy Spirit, how much more glory is available for us today? Paul says that Moses' face would "fade" over time, but the ministry of the Holy Spirit in our lives is "ever-increasing." Could you think of the glory of it? The fire of God in our natural lives should produce ever-increasing evidence of the experience! Because of this, the true believer's life should be filled with the residual colors of God's love, grace, and mercy. This beauty, like that of a sunset, needs no manipulation. They only need to be received and embraced. The afterglow of our encounter with God is ongoing, without end in this life, and it is only by His presence that we do anything productive for the Kingdom of Heaven. We must be ready to shine.

There is another sunset waiting for me. The day is coming when I will leave this world. Whatever light that the Lord shone through my life will eventually dissipate. When the light of my life is turned off, I pray there is an afterglow of a life lived in faithfulness to God. A few have done this, breaking the time barrier and leaving a legacy. Like when the sun sets, a glow can still be found by those who seek it out. A.W. Tozer, F.W. Boreham, Brother Lawrence, Oswald Chambers, and E.M. Bounds are examples of those who have left behind a recorded legacy. They and many others like them have left an ongoing afterglow of faith. They continue to pour into me and inspire me to live Holy, even though all were in the grave well before I was born.

I have learned that God can use the obedient beyond their lives upon this earth. For this reason, I have striven to record documents and journals for my family. I pray that they will impact generations of grandchildren I may never see. I pause here, and I pray for them. I pray they will be blessed with the intimacy I have experienced with this loving and gracious God. I pray that some small record of my life with Him will inspire you to do the same. Always remember that what was poured out on the apostles in the upper room was promised to our children and our children's children and all who are far off! The Spirit is poured out at any moment with those who are "far off" in mind. He has impressed you upon my heart for a reason. Praise God! An afterglow of my life will make an impact!

God has designed and orchestrated all these natural and spiritual phenomena. The ocean, sun, and earth's rotation were all created and set in order by our Creator God. Likewise, the movement of our lives and all the eternal opportunities hidden within each day were prepared for us ahead of time. Just as you can be sure the sun will rise and set in all its glory, you can also be sure that God has prepared work for you today. David writes, *"Your eyes saw my unformed body. All the days ordained for me were written in your book before one of them came to be. How precious to me are your thoughts, O God! How vast is the sum of them"* (Ps. 139:16-17 NIV). Like an awe-inspiring sunset, David realized the omniscient sovereignty of God and His goodness toward us! This God thinks so much of us that He set this day in motion thousands of years before I was born.

Not only has He planned and painted the skies for our blessing and inspiration, but He has orchestrated encounters with Him so that we might know the wonder and majesty of His countenance. No encounter with the Holy Spirit is a chance encounter any more than there is a chance that the sun will rise and set today. Just as natural things were planned and set for us, the spiritual timetable was designed and set for us. Every moment of our lives, good or bad, is being used for His glory. We may not always see it, like the sunset on a cloudy day. It may be obscured, but it is still there. God is working in us and through us.

How do I know? He planned it! Paul reminded the Ephesian church, *"For we are God's workmanship, created in Christ Jesus to do good works, which God prepared in advance for us to do" (Eph. 2:10 NIV).* This sovereign God has planned good works for us today. This is an assurance! Knowing this, we don't have to strive to be used by God any more than we need to strive to find a sunset. We only need to be mindful of the time to catch a sunset and make ourselves available, looking to the west. The same is true of God's eternal work for this day. We only need to be mindful and make ourselves available to His will. Then we will see good or bad moments of our lives are

I will close this chapter out with an example of this sovereignty. One of the greatest subtle mercies the Father has ever taught me was through a man named Todd. My friend, Jeremy Wise, had met Todd at a support group. Jeremy approached me one Sunday and told me he had invited a friend to church. He asked me to be praying for a man named Todd. Todd came up with multiple excuses as to why he shouldn't attend church. The first excuse was that of clothing. He didn't have nice church clothes. Jeremy assured him that clothing doesn't matter at our church. "Some people are dressed up while others come in shorts. Pastor Bob only requires people to come clothed." His next excuse was that he had tattoos in places that couldn't be covered up. Jeremy assured him that no one cared about his tattoos. Todd's last-ditch excuse was his criminal past. He was a felon who was formerly incarcerated and was currently on parole. Again, Jeremy assured him it wouldn't be a problem, especially since his pastor's son was incarcerated at the time. Without any further excuses, he agreed to join Jeremy at church sometime. Todd had seen himself in a church like the mixing of fire and water. They don't usually go together, but God was orchestrating a magnificent expression that would leave us in awe.

The day came, and Todd wasn't hard to pick out. When I saw a big guy with tattoos on his arms and neck walking with Jeremy, I immediately assumed this was Todd, the guy we had been praying for. We had a cordial introduction and some friendly conversation, but then he asked the question, "Jeremy says your son is in prison. Which one is he in?" I answered his question and asked where he was formerly incarcerated. He said he had been in Michigan City. I'll pause and explain that this is notoriously the most brutal prison in Indiana. They don't send petty criminals there. Our conversation continued. I explained to him that I have an uncle that served some time at Michigan City. When he asked me when my uncle had been there, I told him the approximate years. His eyes lit up as he said, "I was there through that time too. Can I ask you his name?" I said, "Chad Woodrow."

I don't know if I can adequately describe the expression on Todd's face. It was somewhere between the fright produced in a funhouse and the surprise of an unexpected gift. Awe overcame him as his mouth dropped open, and his right arm slowly moved toward his left. When he could finally speak, I noticed he was pointing at his left arm, saying, "He did a couple of my tattoos in prison." From that moment, the walls came down. Todd was no longer an outsider or afraid to be at church. The sun had set on the horizon, and the colors were radiant. He belonged in our church as much as the setting sun belongs in the ocean. Fire and water had mixed in a miraculous display of sovereignty. This encounter was not just a coincidence but a God-orchestrated moment.

Todd plugged into our church and started attending our men's discipleship group. He came to faith in Jesus and began ministering to those who had been a part of his old life. He even contacted a man who had grossly sinned against his family in the past so that he could express his forgiveness toward him. These things are signs of genuine conversion. It was one of the most beautiful things I have ever seen or been a part of.

As I observed the glory of God in Todd's life, I didn't realize I was observing a beautiful sunset. A short time later, Todd died from natural causes in his home. Though the sun has set on his life, I marvel at the beautiful afterglow left behind. What a privilege to be able to behold the majesty and sovereignty of God's goodness to orchestrate this moment. Todd was by all accounts a castaway of society, but God orchestrated encounters spanning over a decade that would play a role in his being saved by grace. What are the chances that Todd would end up in a small town with a guy in a group that would invite him to church? Then, the pastor's uncle "just happened" to be in prison with him about twelve years prior and "just happened" to do a couple of his tattoos. The love of God truly is relentless. *"The Lord is not slack concerning His promise, as some count slackness, but is longsuffering toward us, not willing that any should perish but that all should come to repentance" (2 Pet. 3:9 NKJV).*

I am writing this chapter as I sit in Tennessee among towering trees. I am learning today that even the rain has an afterglow. If you are blessed enough to experience heavy rain in a wooded area, you know the storm passes long before the rain ends. I promise it is possible. The sky becomes cloudless after the summer rain has come and gone, but you will become wet as if it were still raining. Those trees! Those precious trees are not just drinking in the rain by the roots, but they act as diffusers, catching the rain, holding it briefly, and then steadily dropping it from leaf to leaf and limb to limb until the drops reach the ground. The rain is no longer there, yet its remnants are evident, just as the clouds in the eastern sky declare the beauty of the sunset.

When I think of Todd's story, it is like the beauty of the eastern sky following sunset and the soothing drips of a refreshing rain that has passed. I stood before his family and friends to minister at his funeral. They heard the account that I shared with you. The afterglow of Todd's life was displayed in a room traditionally associated with sorrow and grief. An unlikely mingling of sin and the blood of Jesus brought forth a testimony of wondrous beauty. Though much of his life had been a storm, when he went to be with Jesus, all that remained was the refreshing drip of the storm's afterglow falling from the trees. Even now, the afterglow of this testimony lives on. It is not different from the woman with the alabaster box. Her story will be told forever.

My thoughts of Todd's story remind me of God's faithfulness. It is easy to be consumed with the ministry, constantly toiling to produce something good. Todd taught me that God is good and has planned good works for me. He does this not because He loves me but because He loves anyone I will encounter on any given day. He has strategically placed us all at this moment for a purpose. His sovereignty has predestined His purpose for us; we only need to be present and available to cooperate with His will. When we do this, something glorious and eternal will take place.